Building
Business-to-Business Relationships
Over the Phone

A case study on developing, nurturing and sustaining
revenue using open-dialogue telephone selling

By John Dieseth
President, Business Performance Group

Business
■Performance Group

For additional copies of this publication,
contact the HRDQ Customer Service Team:

Phone: 800-633-4533 or 610-279-2002
Fax: 610-279-0524
Online: www.HRDQstore.com

ISBN: 978-1-58854-920-4

Publisher: Martin Delahoussaye

Cover image © Brian Jackson / Fotolia.

Printed in the United States of America on recycled paper.

0819E1BK
EN-01-JL-17

Dedication

To Jane, Elizabeth and Anne, who endured
my extended travel along this journey, and
without whose support and love none of this
would have been possible.

Table of Contents

Acknowledgements

I am grateful to all our Business Performance Group clients for their contributions to the art and science of building business-to-business relationships over the phone. Your willingness to try something new, your willingness to learn, and to teach me a thing or two along the way were, and are, appreciated.

A special thanks to Caterpillar and its affiliated dealers. The "Journey to a Billion" was an experience of a lifetime. I worked with thousands of dedicated, intelligent and gifted employees across the globe. All were focused on their customers, mindful of the need to deliver quality each day, and willing to stretch beyond what was done in the past to create a better future. The dealer network is truly a distribution marvel, and is dedicated to serving a complex and demanding market.

And of course, a special thank you to Mark Wankel, my client, my partner and my friend. I can't count the number of times I admired your infinite patience, your political astuteness, and your focused guidance. Whenever a corporate landmine appeared, you steered us clear. Whenever a setback seemed demoralizing, you cheered us on. And whenever creating a billion-dollar initiative seemed like an impossible task, you broke it down into a series of steps we could accomplish.

Thanks to the thousands of telephone salespeople I have worked with over the years. Every call you made enriched my experiences. Each conversation provided further insight into the telephone sales profession, and broadened my knowledge of effective techniques, and what perhaps wouldn't work. Thank you as well to the sales and marketing managers who daily stretch their profession further into the digital age.

Finally, thank you to my wife Jane and daughters, Anne and Elizabeth. You endured my many absences from home while traveling, my alarm ringing at 3:00 in the morning on days I went to Peoria, and the calls from overseas that arrived at all hours. I'm forever grateful for your love and support.

Introduction

Telephone selling to build business-to-business relationships and sales suffers from the reputation of its much less sophisticated and more abrasive relative — telemarketing. The telephone sales representative, unlike the telemarketer, engages in open-dialogue, relationship-building conversations. An observer overhearing this conversation, but not seeing it, would rarely notice a quality difference between the conversation of the field salesperson sitting face-to-face with a customer and the telephone salesperson on the phone. However, since almost everyone has encountered a rude and intrusive telemarketer, in business or in their personal life, the telephone-selling family has acquired an unsavory reputation. Ask anyone whose relative has been involved in an unwholesome activity, and they will tell you the burden a name can carry.

Our team at Business Performance Group ran up against this less-than-stellar reputation as we were developing the inside sales program within the Cat® dealer network. Caterpillar is a Fortune 100 company, listed on the Dow Jones Stock Exchange Index, with a reputation for being progressive and having superior marketing instincts. What started as a skunk works project in Edmonton, Alberta, Canada, has grown globally into a billion-dollar enterprise, deploying hundreds of telephone salespeople. And yes, you can sell heavy machinery and equipment over the phone.

In this book, you'll learn the techniques we use to sell business-to-business using the phone; you'll also learn the inside story of how a cutting-edge-but-mammoth industrial company adopts a new sales platform while overcoming the resistance caused by telephone selling's undeserved reputation.

Caterpillar's business depends not on one-off transactions, but on an annuity stream of business, from equipment sales to parts and service, and then on to the next piece of equipment. Unlike some businesses that can always count on a fresh face appearing on the prospect list, customers who buy power systems and machinery are stable businesses themselves, and there aren't many of them. One bad experience, a broken relationship, or a promise made but not kept, can all hurt deeply. The telephone salesperson, called inside sales representatives or ISRs at Cat dealers, must build a relationship first to qualify to sell these major purchases.

This is a requirement because, though relationship building can come so naturally face-to-face, achieving the same results over the phone takes a special technique.

Think of the last time you were interrupted by a phone call when you were concentrating on something else. Did your mind easily jump to focusing on the telephone conversation? Probably not. The human brain tends to want to keep doing what it's doing, and sees any interruption as an intrusion. Because of this, the telephone salesperson's first responsibility is to generate interest at the beginning of the call. You'll learn how to generate interest on the first call and on each subsequent call, to convince the customer to stop what they're doing and welcome the interruption.

You'll learn how to develop and keep an easy-to-detect business curiosity. Who is most important to you? You, of course! How does the telephone salesperson succeed? By making the call about the customer, not themselves, and this is exceedingly hard. After all, when the salesperson was hired, the selling organization pumped them full of features, drizzled on specials and promotions, and inflated them with motivational pep talks. Why wouldn't they want to talk about themselves and the selling organization? The answer is simple — because it just doesn't work.

You'll also learn how to ask good open-ended questions. Yes, I know, asking open-ended questions is a part of any sales course — been there, done that. But it takes on a different significance when using the telephone, without body language and the conversation starters that the face-to-face salesperson sees in any customer's office or work setting. For the telephone salesperson, open-ended questions take on a whole new meaning, enlarging the conversation to explore beyond what the customer needs right now and uncover business issues that aren't top of mind, but will generate business tomorrow — if we only ask.

We've broken this book into alternating sections. The first section features the case study of our journey at Caterpillar from skunk works to a billion-dollar business, the pitfalls, the politics, the false starts, and the ultimate success. Mark Wankel, who led the effort inside Caterpillar and who has now joined Business Performance Group, will guide us through this thicket. The second section is about the sales techniques that work in a business-to-business telephone selling effort, from relationship building to closing sales. May your journey profit from our experience; experience is the best teacher of course, although she is always the most expensive.

Chapter 1
Check It Out!

Like many good journeys in business, the inside sales journey at Caterpillar began back in 2003 with a difficult business issue: How can dealers cover all their customers cost effectively? Coverage studies showed less than half of customers were assigned to a field salesperson who visited customers face-to-face. These uncovered customers were generating significant business. What would they generate if we paid more attention? Likewise, market share for aftermarket parts and services was far less than desired. What if we could bump these numbers up 10%, or dare to dream, 20%? And how could we make it economical? A field salesperson costs about $600 per visit, given the costs of driving around and the great distances between customers. Many of these customers generated less than $10,000 of parts and service revenue. How many visits could we afford per year at $600 a pop?

At Caterpillar, Mark Wankel faced these issues when he was assigned to participate on a Six Sigma team on customer coverage in 2003. Six Sigma is a set of management techniques and ideas intended to improve business processes, and the Six Sigma process generated the idea of contacting customers over the telephone.

As in many businesses who serve customers in the industrial space, Cat dealers have a parts counter where customers can purchase maintenance supplies and spare parts. These parts counters are staffed by experienced and well-trained parts counter advisors who are experts in uncovering all the seals, gaskets, parts, and maintenance supplies needed for any repair. In response to Mark's Six Sigma analysis, a group of parts counter advisors were selected to call customers when they were not serving customers at their parts desk.

The trial with the parts counter advisors didn't work. A post-mortem showed the parts counter advisors hated making the calls, and would find almost any excuse not to complete them. Also, customers didn't see much value in random calls to see if they needed anything. If they did need anything, they said they'd call the parts counter advisor back or stop by the dealership. A different approach was needed.

Mark and his teammates recognized that the personalities of their salespeople and parts counter advisors were somewhat different, noting this could be part of the problem. They commissioned a study with Caliper, a noted personality-testing organization, to profile field salespeople — both equipment and product support — and parts counter advisors, to create an ideal profile of a telephone salesperson. Not surprisingly, the result of this study showed that parts counter advisors, who had a customer service persona, were not the ideal, although they were perfectly suited for the jobs they were in.

About the same time, Mark's boss Bob Morrison heard of an effort using telephone sales up at Finning Canada, a dealership in Edmonton, Alberta, Canada, and a manager who had come from TELUS, a phone company in western Canada. Bob told Mark, "Check it out!" What Mark discovered and later implemented was the start of a successful B2B telephone sales program at Caterpillar.

Chapter 2
The Relationship Telephone Sales Model

When Business Performance Group first translated our materials to Mandarin, I received a call from the translator who was laughing as we talked on the phone. He was having considerable trouble with the translation of "business relationships," because what kept coming out on paper was the more intimate type of relationships that people create to form new families, and it didn't seem at all appropriate for businesses to be doing something similar to that. He wanted to know exactly what I meant. How can businesses have relationships?

I explained that some firms selling business-to-business have a "one and done product." The product is bought and the buying organization's problem is solved. Other companies that are selling business-to-business seek to acquire an annuity stream of business — a series of transactions over time. They may sell production equipment and then provide maintenance. They may sell an insurance policy and then the renewal. They may do tax services one year, and look forward to the next. This is a business relationship. The telephone salesperson is in the boundary position, between the selling organization and customer, and is seeking to weave the bonds between their organization and the customer so that both parties win, and business continues over time. It is a complex task.

Many functions within companies are somewhat universal to all businesses — for instance, accounting follows generally accepted accounting principles; human resources provides benefits and makes sure everyone plays well in the corporate sandbox. The sales organization, however, may look quite different between firms because of culture, the unique products and services offered, geography, and the impact of various managers. Owners and chief executive officers tend to stir things up in the sales department more often than accounting or human resources, because of the sales group's impact on the top line. Generally, field salespeople juggle between 50 to 150 accounts, and telephone salespeople handle 600 to 800 accounts, but the bell-shaped curve has long tails on both sides. The duration of the typical sales call also has a long tail, but modern field sales calls can last from 20 to 40 minutes, and the length of the business-to-business telephone call may range from 3 minutes to 7 minutes in length. Costs are also important considerations. The cost of an outbound business-to-business telephone sales call can be in the range of $17.00 per call; a field sales call can be $600 per call when you consider all the expenses involved and divide by the number of calls that can be completed in a year.

As a consultant, I've learned you need to understand the culture, the customers, the management, the cost structure, and the legacy of each sales organization.

In the old days, field salespeople would keep the information on each account on index cards somewhere in their car, but most of the information was in their head. Part of their job was carting around information. There was no Internet. The salesperson was the data repository. He or she was welcomed at the customer location because, beyond buying lunch, the field salesperson brought data. If you wondered about the carbon content and tensile strength of a certain grade of bolt, you could just ask the hardware salesperson who would be stopping by the next day.

Today, customers can Google this information and much more (thank you so very much), so salespeople no longer provide data as much as context and insight. For the field salesperson who will have a personal relationship with most if not all their customers, it's a challenge. For the telephone salesperson who will have a personal relationship with far fewer people, it's a mountain to climb.

The second job the field salesperson historically provided was to take orders. Telephone selling grew out of the inside sales order-taker position. Back at the home office, customers could call in between the times the field salesperson stopped by. Today, on-line and automatic ordering systems take over most of this burden — again focusing the sales effort on context and insight.

The best way to provide context and insight is to consult with the customer as long as possible before you begin to sell. Once the salesperson begins to sell, context seems limited to what the selling organization offers, and the salesperson's insight appears limited to what the selling organization has on the shelf.

Our selling model consists of five steps — DISCOVER, DESIGN, DEMONSTRATE, CLOSE, and CHECK. During DISCOVER, the telephone salesperson uncovers business issues that his or her product and services can solve, generates excitement in those products and services and builds the relationship. DESIGN is managing the sales cycle to mirror the buying cycle of the customer and managing a territory much larger than the typical field sales territory. DEMONSTRATE includes product or service presentations that are either conversational or organized around sales collateral. CLOSE is the traditional sales steps of overcoming objections and asking for the sale, and CHECK represents the steps necessary to provide good post-sale customer service and to tee up the next DISCOVER.

By choosing their language carefully, the telephone salesperson can maintain a consulting mindset with the customer through DISCOVER, DESIGN, and DEMONSTRATE, providing context and insight, adjusting the sales cycle as necessary to balance risk and reward, the requirements of the buyer and those around the buyer who may influence the purchasing decision, and meeting the customer's timeline. To do this, the telephone salesperson must take a step up from the historic field salesperson's index cards, and use a good customer relationship management system or CRM. A CRM contains the customer narrative, sales history, key contacts, and influencers and serves as the platform for marketing automation.

A telephone salesperson within an account base of, say, 600 customers may have 40 to 60 sales cycles going at a time, each in different steps of the sales cycle. Perhaps some customers have expressed interest, but now is not the right time. Marketing automation can keep these customers warm between scheduled phone calls. Some customers need information from the telephone salesperson, while others are consulting members of their organization or working to get a purchase order signed.

Following a selling model, juggling hundreds of accounts and dozens of sales cycles, all in various stages, and uncovering business issues that will lead to future sales is challenging. So is building business relationships five minutes at a time. Technique is critically important in telephone sales. One telephone salesperson can decide all they need to do is call people, saying they are "touching base" and take the occasional order. He or she will uncover some business, because they are in the right place at the right time. But the person next to him or her can follow all the right techniques and sell three times as much.

The field salesperson gets credit, as Woody Allen said, in just showing up. The telephone salesperson gets no credit just for showing up. Because they are interrupting the day of their customer. If they add no value, the customer can hold the selling organization in lower regard than they did before the phone rang. This is negative sales pressure, the opposite of what the selling organization hoped to apply. Therefore, poorly designed and executed business-to-business telephone sales efforts fail, often spectacularly. Properly designed and well-executed efforts succeed because a good telephone sales effort will dramatically cut the cost per call, increase customer coverage, produce significant revenue, and build great relationships. Even in Mandarin.

Chapter 3
Bill Buss

In his youth, Bill Buss played semi-professional hockey. A giant of a man, I can't imagine getting driven into the boards by someone his size. Bill has a giant heart to match. For many years, Bill had a quirky friend who ran a restaurant, and one night a customer was giving his friend a bad time and making a scene at the restaurant. Bill simply got up and stood behind him, without his friend knowing it. The unruly customer took the hint and left — Bill's friend none the wiser.

Before joining Finning Canada, the Cat dealer in the western provinces, Bill worked at TELUS Canada in various management positions, as well as freelancing as a management consultant to help businesses start inside sales operations. This brought him to the attention of Finning, and in 2001 he became the inside sales manager and started hiring representatives to sell product support to smaller customers over the phone.

Institutionally, Finning relied on field salespeople, both to sell equipment and to sell product support — parts and service. But Finning's territory was (and still is) immense, stretching from the oil sands in Fort MacMurray to the prairies of southern Alberta. Field sales was a costly effort, and the staff was way too small to cover this geography. Bill discovered thousands of uncovered accounts. He began hiring telephone sales representatives to serve these smaller accounts, growing a staff that in the mid-2000s was more than 20.

Politically, Bill had to stay under the radar as much as possible. Field salespeople were suspicious. Sales were being taken away from them and transferred to telephone sales representatives; these were accounts they didn't call on anyway, but geographically were included in their territory. Telephone sales representatives needed to carefully position themselves as members of a team, to avoid causing customer confusion and incurring the wrath of the machine and equipment salespeople who still sold the big iron.

Bill hired young, hungry, and talented salespeople — and even without knowing the personality profile model Mark Wankel had developed in

Peoria about the same time — salespeople who fit the profile of an ideal telephone sales representative. Bill interviewed all applicants on the phone saying, "If you can't sell yourself on the phone, there is no need to darken my door for a face-to-face interview." As his hiring reputation grew, other managers began seeing his telephone sales representatives as a good farm team, and the average tenure of his representatives became only eighteen months to two years before they moved to management, field sales, or technical pursuits within the dealership. Bill was always hiring.

After about six months in Bill's telephone selling organization, he sent the representatives around to the various other departments of the dealership, to shadow and to see which jobs they might want to apply for in the future. Once they selected an area of focus, Bill began providing each telephone representative with a package of ongoing training, tailored to their desired career path. Bill allowed most of his telephone sales representatives one day a week for ongoing training, shadowing, and learning, knowing that his department was the stepping stone to a career.

In my experience of selling on the phone, in the field and in customer service, telephone selling is the most difficult. In field sales, you are face-to-face and can take advantage of body language. If you work in inbound customer service, the customer is already excited or they wouldn't have called you. With telephone sales, you must generate interest and function without body language. Telephone salespeople usually make excellent field salespeople, and good managers, because they have talked to so many customers and understand the problems, opportunities, and strategies customers face.

Sent by his boss, Bob Morrison, to Edmonton, Mark met Bill and was so impressed by the operation, he hired a film crew to interview Bill and a few other pioneering dealers to create a DVD disk to socialize the concept within the dealer community. Information gathered by interviewing Bill and other dealers was used to create a small Implementation Guidebook, which was given a corporate media number and circulated with the DVD. The goal was to present relationship-building telephone sales as the solution. As they thought about encouraging other dealers to deploy, Mark and his team thought they needed to provide a sales course for telephone salespeople, and a search was launched to find a vendor.

Chapter 4
DISCOVER: Two Sets of Questions

One day I was working in my home office and my wife was at the kitchen table, deep in thought on a work project of her own. Upstairs, my daughter Anne was playing with her friend Kaitlyn, making the kind of noise elementary school girls do when they are having fun. Suddenly, the noise stopped. My wife quickly looked up from her work and said, "Girls, what's happened? Is anything wrong?" That's intuition—a kind of instinctive reasoning honed by experience.

The first step of our model for the relationship-building business-to-business telephone sales representative is to discover openings to position their products or services as solutions. They can't rely on their intuition and make assumptions. If they do, they may waste their own time and the customer's time, proposing a solution of little value. Of course, the salesperson could just dial for dollars, hoping the people they call will have an order they'd like to place. But this type of salesperson will be perceived as a telemarketer, the black sheep of the family, and this approach will result in low sales and low job satisfaction, both for the selling organization and the salesperson. The telephone salesperson also needs to recognize the benefit of having the customer articulate their needs. Once a customer has talked about their needs, they are much more in the mood and motivated to do something about it. Even the experienced salesperson — who has heard it all before — must hear these needs again, both to catch the nuances sheer intuition would miss and to get the customer motivated to move forward.

A business-to-business customer will only buy from a selling organization over time if they have business issues they can solve. When I think about our client base at Business Performance Group, it is easy to see what these business issues are. We have a client that sells artificial limbs and joints. The business issue is within their surgeon customer base, which serves patients whose original body parts aren't working as well as they should. The surgeon wants an effective solution for the patient, and for their practice, reduces time in the operating room and any post-operative problems. We have another client who manufactures forklifts, and customers buy forklifts because they need something with which to move materials. Because the telephone sales representatives we work with want to build relationships that generate an annuity stream of revenues over time, they must be able to uncover these business issues and help customers understand how their solutions can help.

Business issues can be problems, opportunities, or strategies. If you call a customer, they will probably tell you their problems they know you can solve, or may articulate a non-related issue, hoping you can help. At one level, telephone sales is a numbers game, and if you call when a customer has a problem you can solve, you have a good chance of entering a sales cycle you can potentially close.

Opportunities are situations customers are hoping to exploit. For example, a construction company customer may have just been awarded a new project. A bank may have just purchased land to open a new branch office in a growing area of town. A city or town may have just learned a new business is locating inside their corporate limits. Where customers are eager to tell you about problems, they are reluctant to tell you about opportunities — unless you ask, and unless you have a relationship good enough to let you get that close.

Of course, as opportunities get closer, problems pop up and accumulate. The construction company with the new project may need rental equipment, the bank may need a landscaper to sod their new property before the branch is opened, and the city or town may need a lawyer to help rezone the land before the new business relocates. If you uncover an opportunity early — by building the relationship and probing for opportunities during your phone conversations — you may be the rental company, landscaper, or lawyer with the inside track. If you wait, you may be just one of many vendors vying for the business.

A strategy is a customer initiative to improve their business. For example, the customer with construction equipment may desire to reduce their equipment downtime. An office may want to reduce their supplies expense. A bank may want to drive more customers toward automated banking. Strategies are the initiatives customers dream up between Christmas and New Year's Day, or whenever they're considering the future of their business. Think of strategies as the business equivalent of the New Year's resolution.

The telephone sales representative who calls just to "touch base" to see what is going on may hear about any problems the customer has at top of mind. But these are only one third of the business. To learn about opportunities and strategies, the salesperson must ask. The best way to ask is to leverage what you know to discover what you don't know by deploying the salesperson's best friend, the open-ended question. For example, a telephone salesperson calling a construction equipment customer with an opportunity may say, "I understand you were awarded a new project down on Beeker Street. Congratulations! I help customers just like you get their projects done on time and under budget. Tell me about your equipment needs for this project." If the telephone sales representative already has a relationship with this customer, they can open the call, "Congratulations, Sally. I heard you were the low bidder on the Beeker Street project! It looks like a fantastic project. Last time we talked, you said you were evaluating your equipment needs for the season. Tell me what you found."

Strategies are deeper, and customers rarely articulate strategies unless they are comfortable with the relationship. We'll address building a strong relationship over the phone in a later chapter. Open-ended questions work well here, too. For example, "If you could wave your magic wand, what would you change next year in your business," or "When you and your other managers discuss how to improve the business, what changes would you make?" The telephone sales representative who has earned the trust of the customer (and it does not take many calls) will be able to learn customer strategies long before the implementation stage when the details become problems, and the selling organization becomes just another vendor on the request for proposal. The key to being successful is to explore opportunities and strategies with the customer before they become problems.

Once the telephone salesperson has uncovered a relevant business issue, they must determine what product or service they offer that can help the customer address the business issue, and generate sufficient interest so the customer will go through the buying cycle.

During our training sessions, I often ask salespeople, "Who is your biggest competitor?" and I get a variety of responses. But when we examine the actual situation more closely, the real major competitor is usually "do nothing." The customer just continues to do what they've always done. It takes energy to consider a new solution. And as a buyer, they have a process to follow. Something may go wrong along the way, and it takes time. Has anyone ever called someone employed in a business who is not busy? Usually the best buyers are the busiest.

A telephone salesperson selling business-to-business should be increasing their market share within their client base. To do so, the salesperson must get customers to stop buying from competitors in some instances, and in others to get customers to try something new. One of the first rules of physics is an object that is at rest tends to stay at rest. One of the first lessons in sales is that customers tend to keep doing what they have always done. The salesperson's job is to get a "yes" (preferably) or a "no." If you've uncovered a business issue, generated sufficient interest, followed the buying cycle, overcome any objections, and asked for the sale, you have done your job as a salesperson. Sometimes we get a "no," but "no" isn't usually our biggest competitor. "Do nothing" is.

The minute a salesperson uncovers a business issue, and informs the customer they may have a solution, the next step is to generate interest. Interest is the currency the salesperson will use to pay the customer to take the time and energy to go through the buying cycle. What generates interest? Attributes about your product or service that are important to the customer.

My wife came to me one day and said, "I need a new car." Her minivan had just been in the shop, and this had been the final straw for her. So off we went — my two girls, my wife, and me to buy a new car. We decided on a make and model, and two dealerships in Des Moines where we lived offered the vehicle. I was set on getting the best price, my wife on getting a better car. At the first dealership, it went pretty much as you'd expect — salesperson talks about the car, family rides in the car with the salesperson, followed by pressure to commit. At the second dealership, the salesperson walked right up to my wife and started talking to her. Good move. He picked out the buyer immediately — and within two minutes had her sitting in a brand-new SUV, showing her the interior of the vehicle by pointing out the dozen or so cup holders that could be added with an optional center island.

At this point, I was leaning up against the passenger door of the car laughing to myself, because I know that this woman does not believe in eating or drinking in the car. She holds that belief for two reasons, I guess. First, the girls and I spill a great deal, and she wants a clean car. And second, she believes that family meals involve conversation, and conversation is best held around a table, with electronic devices off — not in a car. As we left the dealership that day, I heard, "I am not buying a car with all those cup holders in it!" This is a product objection which the salesperson would not be able to overcome. Now the SUV we did end up buying probably could have had over a dozen cup holders in it, but the salesperson didn't talk about it.

The moral of the story for salespeople is "if you talk about it, it becomes important." Don't cause unnecessary objections, talk about what is important to the customer. What is important generates interest, and if you encounter an objection because of something that is important, it is a true objection, which you need to overcome. Don't create additional objections that aren't important to the customer, but now seem important because you brought them up.

Finding out what attributes are important to your customer is as easy as asking a few questions. Create a matrix with the attributes of your product or service on the left, and questions you can ask to uncover if they're important on the right. For example, say you work for a commercial roofing contractor and you call a building manager. You uncover the business issue that the client has locked in a new tenant to a long-term lease, and they move into the building in two months. They need to repair the roof during this time to assure the new tenant that they will have a worry-free lease. Your proposed replacement roof has a 25-year warranty, backed by both your organization and the supplier, your roofing product provides superior insulation properties which reduces the cost of heating and cooling by an average of 10%, and all your installers are factory trained, drug-free and randomly tested to prove it, and your organization has been around for over 20 years — far longer than your competition. As you can see in the table on the following page, depending on the circumstances, you could ask one of the following questions:

Attribute	Question
25-year warranty	"Is a full warranty on the new roof important to you?"
Insulation – reduce your heating/cooling costs by 10%	"Is reducing your heating and cooling costs important in making your roofing decision?"
Installers factory trained and drug-free	"Is it important the roofing contractor you choose have a professional crew?"
We've been around for over 20 years	"Do you want a contractor who has been doing this for a long time, through good times and bad?" Or, even better: "As you plan your roof repair, what concerns do you have about getting your roof replaced?"

Let's say our telephone salesperson asks these questions and learns: "A warranty is critical. I want to sleep at night knowing this problem is solved," and "No, heating and cooling costs aren't a major concern. I certainly wouldn't pay more for it. The tenant pays the utility bills and they're satisfied with the current level" and "Yes, a professional crew is important. I have other tenants currently in the building, including a lawyer's office, a CPA firm and an interior designer – all professionals" and "My biggest concern is that roof repair is noisy, smelly, dirty and dusty — all big headaches."

The telephone salesperson now uses these answers to generate interest in his or her solution. These attributes become benefits, because the customer has said they're important. The salesperson will probably avoid discussing the heating and cooling attribute, unless he or she can position it as increasing the long-term value of the building, because the customer said it wasn't important. And if the salesperson brings it up, the customer may think they're paying extra for something that is the tenants' concern. The warranty, the 20 years in the business — to reduce the risk of noise, smells, dirt and dust — and the professional crew should generate sufficient interest to keep this telephone salesperson in the customer's buying cycle.

Chapter 5
We Meet

When I've had the privilege of delivering training sessions myself for new Caterpillar ISRs, inevitably someone will ask, "So how did you get started with Caterpillar?" I tell them we cold-called Caterpillar, just like you're prospecting for additional customers on your end. They usually let this soak in for a minute, and then ask how. Hey, I tell them, the process you are learning works.

In the fall of 2004, Business Performance Group began an additional effort to diversify our customer base. Because my background was in engineering and technical sales, we focused originally on manufacturers. This led us to put Caterpillar on our cold-call list. One of our salespeople cold-called into Caterpillar one day and talked to Harold Garrells, who worked for Caterpillar University. Caterpillar University was inward facing and only worked with Caterpillar employees at the time, not customer-facing salespeople, but it was our philosophy that when cold calling, the best thing to do was to find someone within the organization who would talk to you and point you to the decision maker.

I often counsel clients to think of who within their target organizations will talk to you, give you information, and steer you on the right path. It often isn't the decision makers. They may shut you down immediately if you cold call or send you to voicemail or some backwater email address. To generate interest with the decision maker, you need to add value on the call. Often the best way to do this is with some general inside information. Who can provide this to you? In some instances, I've directed clients to call the quality control department.

I am a former ISO 9000 internal auditor, so I know companies may put the quality control department in the back office somewhere, and they don't get many calls from outsiders. But quality control may be able to identify engineering challenges and who is the right person to talk with to propose your organization's solutions. There are many other places to go.

My salesperson suggested I give Harold a call after she did her job and sensed an opportunity. I did and we had a 45-minute conversation. As my salesperson suspected, he did not have an opportunity directly, but he knew of a project over in the Sales Effectiveness group for product support inside sales. If I wanted to come to Peoria, he'd set up a meeting. He also gave me a good idea of the culture within Caterpillar, the reliance on their dealer network to represent the company to customers, the superior engineering that made their products an aspirational brand, and what life was like living in a company town. I'd be more than willing to come to Peoria, exactly four hours away from my home in Des Moines.

In Peoria, I met Mark Wankel, Mike McGarvey, and Larry Czernik in Harold's office. They told me about the Six Sigma projects, the need to increase customer coverage, and the initiative in Edmonton. The business issue was a strategy to increase coverage by using business-to-business telephone selling. At the time, they were looking for a training course to offer to dealers who were hiring these inside sales representatives, or ISRs as they called them. Did we have a training course? Could they see it? Of course they could see it.

I had been working for Rocky White at National Seminars Group in Kansas City for years, almost since I started Business Performance Group. I once ran a seminar company in Kansas City named Seminars International, so I knew all about selling on-site, business-to-business seminars over the phone. When Rocky hired a new telephone salesperson, I came down and did a training session for him or her. I also coached each member of his sales team, which numbered around 20 at the time. Rocky demanded a high-performing sales organization.

If you were in the upper echelon of salespeople, you got a giant framed picture of yourself on the wall. If you were in the lower echelon, you were shown, gently but firmly the door. Rocky also had a background in construction, so I figured he could talk earthmoving with the Caterpillar folks. I asked him if it would be okay if Mark Wankel and Mike McGarvey sat in on the next session. Rocky enthusiastically said yes.

In early May of 2005, Mark and Mike traveled to Kansas City in a driving rainstorm and were greeted by Rocky and myself. Rocky was one of those wonderful clients who became a friend as well as a customer. He rolled out the red carpet, welcoming Caterpillar on the sign in the lobby, and giving them the tour of his National Seminars vast telephone selling organization, the marketing team, and inbound customer service.

I conducted the session and Mark and Mike took notes in the back of the room. Our classroom was full of green but eager newly-minted telephone sales representatives, learning how to sell $3,000 to $100,000 packages of training and products to corporations across the United States. That evening, I took Mike and Mark to dinner, and they talked enthusiastically about the opportunity, but it was way too early to close.

Over the next five weeks, I exchanged emails and telephone calls with Mark, discussing how we would customize the course for Cat dealers, and their investments, schedules, and translations. At the end of this sales cycle, I asked for the sale and was told they had selected our course. On July 22, I met with Mark and Larry Czernik and they told me Bill Buss currently had six telephone representatives in Canada, the dealer in Montreal had two, and the dealer in Louisville, Kentucky had one. And they told me that Bill would be adding six more telephone sales representatives shortly.

Right away, Mark asked me to call Bill Buss up in Canada. I reached Bill on his cell phone as he was driving back to Edmonton from a trip to another branch. We talked for a long time — in fact, until Bill's cell phone battery died and we couldn't talk any more. I took so many notes my hand hurt. I was impressed with what Bill had done with no corporate resources or support.

Mark also asked me to go to Louisville, Kentucky, to see a brand-new salesperson at Whayne Supply, the dealer in that neck of the woods. I left Des Moines just as hurricane Katrina devastated New Orleans and curved northward toward Louisville. As I traveled east and south, in the clear blue sky above me I saw an ominous black circle — Katrina would meet me in Louisville, madly dumping rain the whole time I was there.

Kevin McMurray came from the financial industry but had been on the phone for quite some time selling mortgages before he joined Whayne as their first telephone sales representative, or ISR. Kevin's manager was busy, and Kevin didn't even have a CRM system, but he made the dials. Much of his work that first year was cleaning the database. While I listened, we had calls where we learned a customer had recently died, while other customers were out of business. Some customers thought we were calling to collect money, but other customers were delighted we called — honored in fact.

Kevin barely knew that Cat equipment was yellow, but Kevin sold hundreds of thousands of dollars of new business within the first year, because Kevin knew how to build relationships. Although his product knowledge was limited, he asked good, penetrating questions. He had gatekeepers who stood between him and the decision maker offering cell phone numbers and good times to call. A good telephone sales representative with time in territory has one-third of their calls inbound, from customers they have a relationship with who have a need. Kevin had that in spades.

Chapter 6
DISCOVER: Relationships

As a consumer, each of us has our own revenue (your income) that we use to buy products and services—the everyday stuff you and your family consume. With some of those purchases comes a relationship with the seller. Maybe you always go to the same grocery store because their cashiers are friendly, or you go to the same gas station because the manager gives you a loyalty discount. But what type of relationship do you have with your phone company? Your cable or satellite dish company? Probably small, perhaps microscopic. If another phone company offers a better deal, you're jumping. If another provider of entertainment offers more variety at less cost, you're out of there. But utility and entertainment companies, and even the friendly grocer or gas station owner, have thousands or millions of customers spending a modest amount per year. In business-to-business, the number of customers is usually smaller, and the monetary stakes are much higher.

What manager hasn't turned to his or her salesforce at one time or another and said "we need to build good relationships!" But what does this mean? Does this mean personal relationships, where you know the customer's birthday, children, husband/wife, and what their golf handicap is? Well, that's part of it. Customers buy from people they like. But in business-to-business telephone selling, the second part of relationships is the business relationship—the relationship between the customer's organization and the seller's organization.

Personal relationships tend to be more superficial for telephone sales representatives than field sales. There is an advantage to being face-to-face. Lunch and golf still count. However, the business relationship can be just as strong if the telephone salesperson works hard at it. In any database, it is likely the telephone salesperson will build a personal relationship with maybe 15% of their accounts, but can build a business relationship with far more.

For personality reasons, the telephone salesperson and the customer may just click. If I was working the same territory, I'd connect with a different 15% than you would, because our personalities are different. If you consider the typical telephone sales territory consists of 600 to 800 customers, this means roughly 100 to 120 personal relationships. Another

15% of the database members don't want a relationship at any level. They will transact with the selling organization when they see a need, but they don't desire nor will they participate in a relationship. They just don't want to invest the time or energy to do it, don't see the value of a relationship, or are too wary by nature to get that close to a supplier. The remaining 70% of the typical business-to-business telephone database will not have a personal relationship with the telephone salesperson but may have a business relationship, if the telephone salesperson works at it.

What does a business relationship mean? It means the customer has the selling organization at the top of their mind, and when they have a need that pops up between telephone calls, they pick up the phone and call the telephone salesperson, or shoot them an email, or fire off a text. It means they take the telephone salesperson's call, because they recognize this person adds business value, not just idle chit chat. It means if the telephone salesperson is promoted, and another telephone salesperson takes his or her place, the relationship continues because the relationship is primarily with the selling organization, not the person.

The drawback of establishing and maintaining a business relationship is the institutional memory problem. In most field sales situations, both a personal and business relationship is established — in many cases more personal than business, truthfully, because the parties are face-to-face. When the field salesperson moves on, the personal relationship is disrupted, and the customer naturally expects to start over with their new representative. Competitors will swoop in of course, and try to scavenge off the relationship carcass, and often a transition causes a drop-in market share. How many field salespeople are kept around long after normal retirement age by selling organizations, just to avoid this scenario?

In business-to-business telephone sales, the relationship is more with the business, and less personal, so the relationship lives on when the telephone sales representative moves on, if the institutional memory is well preserved. Of course if not, there can be huge problems. For example, if the customer has articulated their problems, opportunities, and strategies to the telephone sales representative, and they have a business relationship (70% of the customer database) and not personal (15% of the customer database), the customer will assume a brand-new representative will know these problems, opportunities and strategies, because they have articulated these business issues to the selling organization.

If the telephone sales representative does not take good notes and construct an easy-to-understand customer narrative, the business relationship can be ruined, and the customer will be put into play unnecessarily. This narrative is not just necessary for a new person coming in to the territory, but for the existing salesperson as well. With a territory of 800 customers, the telephone sales representative will be juggling some 560 (70%) business relationships and 120 (15%) personal relationships. How can they keep this all in their head?

I encourage managers to audit the customer narratives of their telephone salespeople. Study them. If you were a new representative, would you be able to read the narrative and pick up the business relationship? If you can't, you need to counsel the salesperson to take better notes. If the salesperson is not a fast typist, have them leave to-the-point audio notes to document what they uncover. The better the telephone salesperson, the more they will uncover, and the better documentation they will need for themselves and their eventual replacement.

From one manager to another, let me give you a little reminder of salesperson psychology. As an employee that can be held personally responsible for results, a salesperson is always a little on edge in terms of job security. Holding customer information close to the vest, in their head, and not in the customer narrative, is a way of hedging that job security.

"They can't fire me," the salesperson thinks. "I know too much about my customers. They'll lose business." This is true in any sales role of course, and it is an inevitable part of field sales, where the territories are smaller and the personal relationships deeper. With telephone salespeople, you can minimize this problem by providing career paths, encouraging learning that points the telephone salesperson toward growth, having an honest and open relationship with everyone so they know where they stand, and by providing good emotional nutrition.

If you are a manager experienced with field sales, you'll find managing telephone salespeople a totally different experience. Field salespeople gain emotional energy from their customers in the field and from their personal relationships. Telephone salespeople invest emotional energy all day long, and because only 15% of their database is personal relationships, emotional re-charges are few and far between. Being on the phone all day is emotionally draining. Because of this, the manager of a telephone sales organization selling business-to-business can expect to be required to provide emotional nutrition—"Atta girl/Atta boy," and rah-rah sales meetings. The manager must allow venting when needed, contests when desirable, and be always supportive.

Business relationship building begins with asking good, opened-ended questions and having a genuine business curiosity. When telephone salespeople learn about the product, when they learn how to manage a sales cycle, and when they learn how to overcome objections, they learn approaches that work with most of their customers. After all, product knowledge has applicability across their customer base. But relationship building is unique, and depends on the personnel, the marketplace, and the aspirations of each individual customer. Each customer is unique.

Business curiosity is: 1) the telephone salesperson's personality — having sufficient empathy to want to know how each individual customer ticks, and 2) knowing the mechanics of how to build a relationship on the phone. The hiring part will be covered in a future chapter. The "how to build a relationship" consists of asking three series of good, open-ended questions.

The first series of questions concerns how they would use what the selling organization is providing, or would like to provide, to the customer's business. For example, one of the products Caterpillar provides is a standby generator for large buildings. So in case the power goes out, the lights don't. A way to express your business curiosity is to ask, "Tell me about the tenants who occupy the building the generator protects." Or, as another example, we have a client that manufactures production machinery for beverage packaging, so a question that expresses business curiosity might be, "Tell me about the beverages you package, and what markets you serve." The goal is to ask a question as close to your product or service offering as you can, so it seems natural to the customer that you would be curious.

The second series of questions allows you to expand from this narrow focus to find out a little more about what makes the customer's business tick. The first series was narrowly constructed around what the selling organization provides, and the next question is about the customer's business in general. In the case of the standby generator, a follow-up question might be, "It sounds like you have a diverse group of tenants in this building. How do you balance the needs of so many kinds of leaseholders?" Or, in the case of the production machinery, "Give me an idea of how you decide which beverages to offer." These are ways of broadening the conversation to find out more of why the customer does what the customer does. What makes them unique? How do they approach their market?

Finally, the third series of questions is about the buyer, personally. Because you are calling over the phone and can't see the customer, a telephone representative needs to be careful not to pretend a false sense of intimacy exists. How many times have you had a telemarketer ask you, "How are you doing today?" Does the telemarketer really care? If you blurted out a litany of woes sufficient to weave into a good Country Western song, would the telemarketer even notice? Of course not. It's a throw-away line, a false sense of intimacy. The best thing to do is to leverage your discussion about the business to ask what the customer does within the business. For example, "It sounds like you have a fascinating business. What are your responsibilities?" Take your cue from their response.

Building a business relationship is like peeling an onion. On the next call, the telephone representative should ask themselves, "What do I know about how they use products and services like ours, their business, and about them personally? What additional questions can I ask to go a little deeper?"

The best time to write these questions is just after you complete the last call. If the salesperson constructs the questions just after they get off the call and puts them in their customer narrative, the questions will be available in their notes the next time they call.

Other questions telephone sales representatives will create will revolve around the product and business issues that may be used with multiple customers. The relationship-building questions are unique to the specific customer. This requires substantial discipline, commitment to detail, and salesperson-organizational prowess to pull off. It requires a keen business curiosity. The representative must really want to find out what makes the customer's organization tick. Some business curiosity can be taught, but a large part of business curiosity is personality. Sales managers should keep this in mind when selecting telephone salespeople to join their organization. Telephone salespeople calling business-to-business normally juggle between 600 and 800 customers. This means they are also juggling 600 to 800 unique and culturally different relationships.

Remember, customers will recall the conversation with the telephone representative more than the telephone representative will remember the conversation with the customer. To the customer, the telephone representative is one of a limited number of vendors they talk to. On the other hand, for the telephone sales representative, this customer may be one out of 800. Building a good relationship includes keeping good and careful notes in the customer narrative, so the salesperson can keep each customer straight. When I was on the phone, my least favorite moments were inbound calls from Bob or Mike or Sue. I had dozens of each of these common names in my database, and it took a few moments for my brain to pick out the specific Bob or Mike or Sue that was calling.

One of the best days of my life was when we obtained software that automatically pulled up the customer record from my database using the caller I.D. This problem becomes more acute the more the representative builds their customer business relationships of course. As customers divulge more and more intimate details of their use of products and services, their business, and themselves, they will respond more intimately on subsequent phone calls.

What then is the sign that telephone salespeople are building good relationships? Inbound calls. A good telephone sales representative with time in territory should expect about one out of three calls are inbound – where a customer calls them. They call because of the relationship, because they hope the telephone sales representative can help them. Many of the conversations begin with, "I was wondering if you folks could help us with this?" And the answer is, "Of course we can, and we will."

Once the selling organization gets good at asking these additional questions, and the staff has a culture of business curiosity, the sales manager should ask, "How deep should we build these relationships?" This is not an easy answer. Building a relationship takes time. For each account, the manager must decide whether their goal is to be a "trusted vendor" with limited market share, or if the goal is to be a "business partner" with dominant market share. It may vary from account to account based on the opportunity the selling organization may realize.

The manager should ask, "Can revenue be increased from the account by applying additional sales pressure and making the transition from trusted vendor to business partner?" The manager may have intangible factors come into play, such as, "Do we want to invest the time to become a business partner?" or "Do we have the resources to be a business partner?"

Years ago, I was in the steel fabrication business, and I had three steel warehouses who were trusted vendors. I bought about $10,000 worth of steel a week, and typically I knew who had the cheapest flats, I-beams, pipes, or rounds. Every couple of months, I would query all three on a larger order, just to make sure I knew the pricing array. Everyone had a field salesperson who called on me, and an inside representative who did the same. Is this the goal of your selling organization? To be always in the mix, to be on the short list, to always get the request for proposal, or do you desire a deeper relationship?

In many instances, a trusted vendor will hit a selling wall where the customer will feel uncomfortable increasing the market share beyond a certain point, usually less than 50% of the total opportunity. This is because, beyond this point, the customer feels they are losing the chance to play one vendor against the others, and they may be concerned their ability to price discover by soliciting bids from multiple sources will be compromised.

A "business partnership" has the benefit of ushering the customer to where he/she is not afraid to commit more than 50% of the available opportunity. A business partnership is highlighted by long-term and extensive operational ties, and both buyer and supplier do not act as adversaries. Both parties share in the commercial value the partnership creates. In this case, the supplier is not forced to bid against other suppliers continually, because beyond the product and/or service, there is inherent value in the relationship.

For example, a commercial building owner may hire a security firm who establishes significant infrastructure within the facility to protect it, or a large company may outsource most of their human resource and benefits function. These types of relationships require more care and nurturing, but the commercial returns are huge. Within a business partnership, a telephone sales representative may have help from field sales, customer service, and operational departments.

For the manager, the ultimate decision is what type of relationship is desirable, given the selling organization's mix of products and services. In some cases, being a trusted vendor is the best you can hope for. In other cases, without a business partnership, the selling organization can't thrive. Whatever the selling organization's choice, it drives the activity level, the type of individuals hired, and the management of the sales organization.

Can a "business partnership" be built over the phone? Yes, and technology helps. Phone calls can be enhanced using technology such as Skype, which allow for a face-to-face experience. If the sales manager targets accounts to develop into partnerships, the telephone sales representative will need to invest more time in fewer accounts. The planned annual rate of call (PAR) will climb, the number of contacts at each organization will grow, and the complexity of account management will increase.

Consider who "counts" as a business partner for you? Who invests considerable time in building a relationship with you, nurturing the relationship, creating a bond? For most consumers, the best examples are providers of financial products and insurance. Unlike the cable company or grocery store, each customer of the insurance agent or financial planner is financially important, and the delivery of their service requires a good deal of trust. Most consumers have "my financial planner" or "my insurance agent" and these businesses have a high market share of the consumer's business.

For the selling organization, it may be enough to be a "trusted vendor." The telephone salesperson can call outbound four times a year, ask relationship-building questions, and express business curiosity, thereby maximizing potential market share. In other cases, a "business partnership" is desired, and the organization will need to devote considerably more sales energy.

Regardless of the choice, relationship building is a key component of telephone sales. Relationship building sets telephone sales apart from telemarketing. It humanizes the selling organization and uncovers long-term customer opportunities and strategies.

This type of synergy doesn't happen by itself. What sales manager hasn't said "build good relationships" to their team? The key is to hire the right people, coach and train, and define and manage to the level of relationship, which maximizes the effectiveness of the selling organization.

Chapter 7
Deployment Issues

How can I describe Jackie?

Spitfire. Ball of energy. The Energizer battery with a lithium ion backpack.

I was invited to attend a Caterpillar ISR Dealer Exchange, a gathering of dealers to share best practices, in Peoria during the fall of 2005. We met at the Par-A-Dice Motel in Peoria, which is nestled along the Illinois River. Jackie was a Caterpillar representative for North America and was hosting the event. Mark had invited me to attend and present some information on our training courses, and to discuss implementation challenges dealers might face in rolling out the ISR program. As I entered the ballroom, Jackie took one quick look at me, asked me my name, immediately located my name on the agenda, and said "sit here." I did. The dealers were arranged on a "U" shaped table with the Caterpillar folks; I, as a mere consultant, was at the back.

The meeting kicked off with a short presentation by Caterpillar, explaining the strategy, and continued with four dealers who had deployed telephone sales representatives. They presented where they were with the program, the challenges they faced, the struggles they were overcoming, and the revenue generation that made it all worthwhile. Bill Buss had a conflict, and he didn't attend, but almost every other pioneer was there. Sixteen other dealers attended who were evaluating the program, but had not decided yet to deploy.

Jackie ran the meeting like a kindly drill sergeant, friendly but persistent, keeping everyone on time. And if anyone made a mildly disparaging comment about the corporate office, she was there with an equally penetrating comment about the dealers. Almost all the managers in attendance had come from a field sales background, meeting customers face-to-face. They were promoted because they were the best, and you could tell they missed the daily interaction with customers. They knew they had to adopt a different selling strategy for smaller accounts; they knew that coverage was lacking and tens of thousands of customers were uncovered by salespeople. Yet there was a hesitancy and reluctance to embrace telephone sales. The elephant in the room was the ghost of the telemarketer, lurking in the shadows.

I was up right after lunch. As an outsider, I tried to reduce their fears with success stories from our practice. I told them about making sure their telephone sales representatives engaged the customer immediately. I told them the first call would be to introduce themselves, and all future calls would be about the customer, beginning with something from the customer narrative. I told them one third of their calls should be inbound — because that way we'll build relationships. A telemarketer would never do that. As I sat down, Jim Durrett from Whayne Supply, who I had met when I visited Kevin McMurray, turned to me and said, "Great presentation. What did you ever do to Jackie to get the slot right after lunch?" He smiled and patted me on the back. Welcome to the dealer network.

During a dinner the first night of the two-day exchange, I sat by representatives of a western dealership. They had a rural territory, hundreds of square miles, often dotted with ranches with a few pieces of Cat equipment. They had loyal customers — but the area was prohibitively expensive to cover by putting someone in a pickup and asking them to visit. Yet they wanted that next sale of equipment, and they wanted the parts and service business in between. Could this coverage model work for them?

Also at the same table was a metro dealer, located in a huge southern city. They laughed, noticing they had the same problems, but for another reason. They had thousands of small customers — landscapers, small contractors, small governmental units — and because of traffic, it took forever to get from one to another by pickup, even though it may be just a few miles. And some of their customers only spoke Spanish, and serving these customers was difficult. But these customers too were loyal. The dealership wanted the next sale, and to support the equipment the customers had. Would telephone sales work for them and for their dealership?

At the end of the exchange, the pioneers of the concept had shared their experiences — the arrows they'd taken in the back along the way as well as the successes they'd had. Mark went to the flip chart and gathered dealer concerns:

- How do we consistently hire the right person?
- How can we use the ISR program to groom future field salespeople?
- How much time on the phone is relationship building and how much is sales?
- How do we train and orient our ISRs?
- How do we manage ISRs?
- How many do we need?

Many dealers were reluctant to deploy this new sales platform. It was new. It wasn't face-to-face. The specter of telemarketing haunted them. The thought of all these young millennial salespeople flooding the dealership with little or no product, sales, or industry knowledge seemed overwhelming.

As I met with Mark and his team afterwards, we talked about how to socialize the ISR concept across the dealer network — about the "buying cycle" or perhaps the "buying-in cycle" of the dealers. They knew there was an issue — coverage. They were gathering information now, deciding what to do. Option evaluation and the decision to plunge ahead — to buy-in and do it — was still in the future. We had to sell the concept. But we'd uncovered a business issue and generated interest in the initiative; we had a good business relationship. The joking, the sharing, and comradery showed that was true.

We had a sales cycle.

Chapter 8
DESIGN: Sales Cycles

Think of a time you bought something big for you and your budget. It might have been a car or a house, perhaps a dream-of-a-lifetime vacation. What sequence of events did you go through to decide to buy this large-ticket item? You probably decided what you wanted to do, did some research online and maybe consulted with friends and family. You made a list of options, evaluated each, worried about the investment in making your purchase, made a choice, and bought. Afterwards, in the driver's seat of your new car, the comfort of your new home or on an idyllic beach somewhere, you evaluated your decision to buy and asked "was this what I was expecting?"

Just like you, buyers in business-to-business typically go through steps to make a purchasing decision:

1. Needs Definition: How do I take this business issue I'm having (problem, opportunity, or strategy) and solve it. Can I purchase something that will solve it?

2. Information Search: I guess I've decided I can purchase a solution. Where do I look? Who are my possible vendors or business partners?

3. Option Evaluation: How can I evaluate all these solutions available to me to determine the best one to buy?

4. Risk Evaluation: What can go wrong in either my solution selection process or with the solution once I buy it?

5. Decision: I need to make up my mind.

6. Post-Purchase Evaluation: Did I make the right decision?

Some purchases that involve low-dollar amounts or repetitive buying may skip some or all of these steps and go quickly to decision. But for new offerings, especially for opportunities or strategies, buyers will likely go through a process like this. For the telephone salesperson to be successful, they must have conducted a parallel selling cycle to match the buyer's buying cycle. The selling cycle and buying cycle together comprise the sales cycle. The questioning process discussed in Chapter 4 will assist the customer in Step 1, Needs Definition, and it will provide the salesperson with a list of the attributes of their product or service which are of interest to the buyer.

During Step 2, Information Search, the salesperson may provide supportive literature, case studies, references, white papers, demonstrations, trials, or whatever else will assist the customer in their information search. For larger purchases, with substantial risk, perhaps the salesperson can offer a plant or facility tour as appropriate.

During Step 3, Option Evaluation, the salesperson should consider providing the customer with at least three options if possible. The telephone salesperson is positioned well if the option evaluation is between three alternatives he or she has presented rather than three vendors, of which his organization is just one.

During Step 4, Risk Evaluation, the salesperson should be doing everything possible to reduce the risk profile of what they are offering. Are there people within the selling organization the buyer should meet? Are there warranties or guarantees the selling organization can offer? Risk is defined in this context as "the possible impact on the business times the uncertainty." (Risk = impact on the business x uncertainty.) The telephone salesperson can either reduce the possible impact on the business (warranties, guarantees) or the uncertainty (references, case studies, testimonials), or preferably both.

During Step 5, Decision, the salesperson must ask for the sale.

During Step 6, Post-Purchase Evaluation, the telephone salesperson should check back with the customer to make sure everything went as planned.

Time kills all deals. You've probably heard that as well, but rushing faster than the customer is willing to go will result in the stall, where the salesperson doesn't get a "yes" or a "no," and the customer stops taking his or her call. Each sales cycle must end with either a "yes," a "no," or a "no decision," where the sales cycle stalls out before a "yes" or "no" is achieved. The telephone salesperson's job is to get a "yes" or a "no" — preferably more "yes" than "no" of course. But sometimes what the selling organization is offering may not be the best fit, the best price, or the best solution, so sometimes "no" is the answer. Of course, if the salesperson never got a "no," you'd have to wonder why we have them in the first place. If the product is so popular everyone buys it, just put up a simple website and take orders. Competition is good in most industries. A "no" is possible.

A "no" may be a product problem, a price problem, a supply problem, or perhaps the salesperson didn't sell using the best technique, but a stall is usually a salesperson problem. The salesperson's job is to run the sales cycle in such a way that a decision is reached after careful consideration.

Most telephone salespeople find it is not the "no" answers that rob the most sales. It is the stall.

The second sales cycle problem is one of participation. How many of the possible sales cycles within the telephone salesperson's territory is he or she participating in? In a typical scenario, a selling organization may be participating in 30% of the possible sales. If the salesperson's closing ratio is 20% of the sales cycles they participate in, the selling organization will realize 6% of the sales potential in the territory, or will have 6% market share. If the salesperson builds good relationships, and participation rises to 60%, which is totally doable, the salesperson will deliver a 12% market share — double. But if the salesperson focuses on their selling skills only, and doesn't worry about the business relationships they are building, and raises their close percentage to 30% — half again as many sales closed, a monumental achievement — the resulting market share will be 9%. In a typical selling situation, it is easier for a new telephone salesperson to build business relationships to the point that participation rises quickly, than to hone and refine their selling skills to the point where they can close half again as many sales. Work on both, but don't forget the math.

To manage a sales cycle, the telephone salesperson needs to manage and ask questions around the need requirements, buying committee, risk, and timeline. Remember, the salesperson generated interest earlier by finding attributes of their product or service that were exciting to the customer. This is the currency they will now draw upon to maintain enough energy to get to the finish line, the close. To the buyer, need requirements, buying committee, risk, and timeline are boring, and energy stealers. However, to the telephone salesperson, they are mandatory to manage the sales cycle and to avoid a stall.

The need requirements are the details the telephone salesperson needs to fulfill the order. The "why" has already been answered — the "why" is the business issue. Needs requirements answer "who" — who will need to provide information or be involved in the purchase details? (Not who will influence the purchasing decision. This is addressed in buying committee.) "What" — Do you need serial numbers, any specifications to complete a quotation? "Where" — Where does the product need to be delivered? Need requirements are the nitty gritty.

The buying committee is made up of the individuals within the customer's organization who will influence which solution will be purchased. Some customer organizations have formal buying committees. Others rely on informal networks. And in small companies, the buyer may rely on their spouse or other relative. The goal of the telephone salesperson is to identify who will be participating in the decision-making process, and to gain the permission of their contact to talk to them if possible. Why? Because your contact, regardless of how dedicated they are, is not a salesperson. They will forget key benefits of your solution, mishandle objections, cave at the slightest resistance, and tack to the prevailing political winds. The telephone salesperson shouldn't abdicate his or her selling responsibility.

As the salesperson identifies and contacts each member of the buying committee, they need to go through the discovery process once again, beginning with the business issue. Every member of the buying committee may identify the issue slightly differently. Some may not even recognize the business issue. On many occasions, I have been surprised when members of the buying committee were unaware of the magnitude of the business issue facing my primary contact. As they prequalify attributes of their solution to produce a list of benefits, they may have a different list with each contact. This will not only allow the salesperson to generate excitement with everyone, but it also broadens the list of benefits for any group presentations.

While discussing the buying committee with the customer, the telephone sales representative should probe for the customer's buying expectations. Customers have both needs and expectations that arise from any encounter with a member of the selling organization. Customer needs are usually tangible, and earlier in this course I presented how a telephone sales representative could probe for those needs and later need requirements.

Customer expectations are often intangible. Expectations center on how any contact with the selling organization is managed and handled, and how any issues raised during the contact are addressed. Expectations of the customer include: being treated with respect, treated professionally, listened to, cared for, appreciated, and having gratitude expressed for their business.

When discussing the buying committee with the buyer, the telephone sales representative can broaden the discussion to include any questions regarding customer expectations. These expectations may be sensitized by an encounter with a competitor, either for good or ill. By discussing expectations during the buying committee discussion, the representative can make it less personal, and therefore they are more likely to get an honest answer.

For example, "If you decide to move forward with our firm, I want to ensure the buying experience exceeds your expectations. When your organization has made purchases like our product or service in the past, what happened during the purchasing process that was a challenge to you? And what went well? What are your expectations?" This is a natural byproduct of the discussion on who else is involved in the buying process, even if the customer comes back and says they are the only decision maker.

The next, and most ignored, set of questions in the sales cycle is risk. Why doesn't the customer take your call after you have sent out a proposal? They are pondering risk – what can go wrong (e.g., am I paying too much money, what if the selling organization goes away, what if my salesperson goes away, can I trust them, do I like them?) Because I'm an engineer by original training, it is my pleasure to introduce a mathematical equation here for you to ponder: risk = uncertainty x the impact on the business. There is no risk if there is no uncertainty. Something you know will happen may spur an objection, but it is not a risk. Something which has no impact on the business also is not risky.

The equation indicates the best way to deal with risk is to either reduce the uncertainty, or reduce the impact on the business. Warranties and guarantees reduce the impact on the business. If the customer is worried what the telephone salesperson is selling them may break down, a warranty or guarantee reduces the impact on the business. You may offer a pilot program that allows the customer to "dip their toe in the water" and try your product or service without a full conversion. Uncertainties can be addressed with references, case studies, independent verifications, tours of your facilities, and other techniques. The branding of the selling organization reduces uncertainty. If customers trust the brand, they may trust the selling organization.

Most telephone salespeople are charged with taking market share away from the competition. To do so, the customer must drop who they are buying from now, and buy from the selling organization. This is risky. Even if the entrenched competitor is providing inferior products or services, even if the competitor's customer service leaves something to be desired, even if the competitor's salesperson is hard to trust – it is the devil the customer knows.

Business entities are, in general, more risk averse than consumers because of the dynamics of corporate buying. Think of yourself as a buyer in a typical corporation. You need to buy a certain product or service, and for many years you have been buying from supplier "Y." Along comes a new telephone salesperson, and demonstrates their product or service is superior to supplier "Y;" perhaps it costs less, perhaps it performs better, or perhaps the other customers of the new telephone salesperson's offering just rave about it.

As the buyer considers switching vendors, don't you think they consider a point like, "Well, if I stay with supplier 'Y' no one will challenge me, because we've been doing it for years. If I switch to the company represented by this new telephone salesperson, and something goes wrong, it's my head on the chopping block." The uncertainty of switching causes the buyer to pause, and the sale stalls.

The best way to avoid this problem is to get the uncertainties out on the table and make them less uncertain, and to reduce any impact on the business. The first step is to ask risk-based questions to find out what uncertainties they have, and what the impacts on the business are.

Back in DISCOVER, the telephone salesperson probed for the business issue: a problem, an opportunity or a strategy. An opportunity or a strategy may be a "green field" where there is no entrenched competition because the opportunity or strategy may be brand new. In this case, the salesperson may be selling against other potential vendors, but not against entrenched competition. With problems, it may be a problem with an existing supplier that is causing the customer to look around. Either way, whether going against entrenched competition or plowing a green field, elements of risk are present.

"Tell me what you like or dislike about your current supplier." If the customer has a current entrenched supplier, this type of question may uncover uncertainties; it may also uncover attributes of your product or service that can become a benefit.

"As you consider buying 'x,' what concerns do you have about moving forward?" A question like this may uncover uncertainties. "If you could wave your magic wand, what would you do?" or "When you are thinking of buying 'x,' what keeps you up at night?"

Questions like these may also uncover impacts on the business the salesperson didn't think about or uncertainties that keep them tossing and turning.

I've listened to over 13,600 telephone sales conversations. In less than 15% of the calls, the telephone salesperson probes for elements of risk. But the 15% who do are top performers. Earlier we talked about building relationships. Do you have a good relationship with your customer? Have you shown a business curiosity to demonstrate you really care about improving their business? Have you really tried to understand them? If so, they will tell you their uncertainties.

I recently traveled to Australia on business. The lady who sat next to me on the plane was terrified of flying over water because of the Malaysia

Airlines flight that disappeared into the Indian Ocean. Well, the Pacific is a big ocean, and on the way from Los Angeles to Melbourne, it is water for a clear majority of the flight. This gal stayed awake, fretting until we came over the coast of Australia, and then promptly fell asleep, even though the statistical odds of disappearing into the ocean are vanishingly small.

Thousands die in our country each year from the flu. Many people don't get vaccinated against flu even though it reduces the odds of getting sick. But if a virus or another rare disease pops up in a distant continent, even though the chance of getting the disease is remote, it will be featured on the news each night and many people will be much more frightened of this new disease than the flu. This is because the flu has always been with us, even though the danger of this new disease is much less. This demonstrates that humans are not always rational. As such, do not think business buyers' risk analysis is always rational.

They are the same human beings that freak out when a new virus is discovered. It is often easier to accept the problems they know than to take a leap into the unknown. Ask the questions; uncover the uncertainties and the impacts on the business. To all of you telephone salespeople, deal with risk. It's part of your job. It's what you get paid for. Websites can take orders.

Now we move on to the timeline, which answers the question "when?" The telephone salesperson already has their own timeline; it is "right now" or at least "before the end of the month." Customers operate differently. Each business issue has a timeline driven by the needs of their business. For example, if the telephone salesperson is selling liability and workman's compensation insurance, the natural deadline will be when the customer's current liability and workman's compensation policies expire. The customer will have little sense of urgency prior to this.

The first chore in establishing a timeline is to probe for the business drivers. When does the customer need your solution? Once you have that date, it is best to probe backwards to determine a logical decision date. Going back to our earlier example, the salesperson could ask, "You said your current policies expire at the end of March. If you decide to purchase from our agency, we could need a couple of weeks to get everything set up. Could you make a decision by March 15th?" The customer will either say yes, or the customer will give you an alternate date.

The next question should align the salesperson with the customer's information search and option evaluation, "To make a good decision by

March 15th, if I get you a complete quotation and description of our policies choices by March 1st, does that give you enough time for evaluation before your decision date?" The customer will confirm this date, or give you another. Either way, you have a date.

The salesperson can then say, "When I work with other customers, I usually go through a few steps to assure I get them the most cost effective and least paperwork-intensive insurance options. First, I'd like to get information on your payroll and job classifications. This will help me determine the appropriate classifications for workman's compensation purposes. Second, I have a questionnaire I need to complete for the underwriters to get you a quotation on liability insurance. You also said you wanted to visit our offices, to get to know us, and I'll set up a tour for you. You also said you wanted a highly-rated carrier, so I'll provide you the government's rating on our business. You said you wanted references. I will provide you three references of firms I work with, and if you would like more, just let me know. I'd be happy to provide them. Finally, I'll provide you with a quotation, and call you to review the quote and make sure I answer any questions you might have."

In my example, the telephone salesperson just set up a sales cycle with the following steps:

1. Gathering information on payroll and job classifications

2. Answering the questionnaire on liability insurance

3. Visiting the selling organization's office

4. Providing information on the selling organization's financial rating

5. Providing three references — more if asked

6. Providing a quotation — and reviewing it with the customer

Where did all this come from? From the needs identification process and probing for need requirements, buying committee, and risk. If the salesperson learns of more risk or need elements from other members of the buying committee, these would be added to the sales cycle.

Setting a timeline with the customer and defining the steps of the sales cycle has four major benefits for the telephone salesperson. First, when does the customer expect the salesperson to ask for the sale? On the decision date, they've already agreed the customer will make up their mind on or around this date. Between now and then, therefore, the salesperson can be a consultant, not a salesperson. The customer will relax because he or she already knows when the salesperson will try to close; in the meantime, they can work with the consultant to get all these steps done — even though these are the same person. This is a huge benefit to the salesperson. With their consultant hat on, the telephone salesperson can continue to discover potential objections, risks, additional needs and can uncover more attributes of their product that will be benefit to the buyer.

The second benefit of defining the timeline is what will happen to a competitor who arrives on the scene at Step 3? In the back of his or her mind, the customer will probably think, "You're too late! To make a good decision, I need to go through at least six steps and I don't have time to go through them all with you now. I think what I'll do is get a quote from this person just to keep everyone honest."

So, the customer has recruited a competitor to make sure the selling organization of the telephone salesperson is providing a fair price. This is called "column fodder" because many customers will put together a spreadsheet of their proposed investment and one of the columns will consist of this latecomer. Who is in the driver's seat? The telephone salesperson who defined the logical timeline. Who will get the last look? That's right, our hero.

The third benefit of defining the timeline is back to risk. When is the customer most consumed by risk, most worried? Right before the decision date. Think of the last time you bought anything expensive, perhaps a house or a car. As the seller slid those documents over to you and asked for your signature, you may have been thinking, "Boy, I can't wait to walk into my new home," or "I can't wait to get these wheels on the road." Or you may have thought, "I sure hope I can make the payments." Most buyers get all tied up in evaluating risk at the end of the sales cycle, right at the decision date.

The fourth benefit is this — a timeline makes the sales cycle about the buyer, not about the seller. In our example, the telephone salesperson should close the first call by asking the closed-ended question, "May I set up this process for you?" or something similar. The customer will say yes because this whole process sounds like a reasonable process to make a good decision, and may ask for additional steps if they feel there is a need. On the next call, the telephone salesperson can open the call by saying, "You asked me to give you a call today to gather information on payroll and job classifications, and to answer the questionnaire on liability insurance to enable you to make a good decision on your upcoming insurance renewal." Because the telephone salesperson closed the customer on the timeline, all the steps of the timeline are about the customer, not the selling organization.

Let's word it differently: "I'm calling today to get some information from you on your payroll and job classifications, and to fill out this liability questionnaire I have here." Yawn. Everything you've said is about the selling organization. The customer's day is interrupted and is now less than enthusiastic. The energy has ebbed and all future calls will be directed to voicemail. Of course, the object of the call is the same either way, but by closing on the timeline, the focus is clearly on the customer's needs to make a good decision, and who out there in business-to-business land is not interested in making a good decision?

The telephone salesperson is the consultant, the facilitator if you will, of the customer's buying process — not an adversary, not a pest, not a hindrance. The second wording is about the selling organization's need to make a sale, not the buyer's need to make a good decision. This second approach makes it easy for the sales process to stall out. The buyer may think, "This is too much work, I'll just renew the policy I have." When the call begins with, "You asked me," the buyer sits up straight, thinks to themselves, "You bet I did," and the sales process moves on.

By defining a timeline, the telephone salesperson has conveniently allocated this customer's risk analysis phase to a defined date, in our example, March 15th. But the sales cycle is completed once the customer has the quote and the salesperson has reviewed the quote with the customer. What a perfect time to ask for the sale, before the customer is deep in risk analysis. The salesperson can review the quote, make a recommendation (we'll call this a business proposal later), and ask for the sale by saying, "Is there any reason we shouldn't move forward?" If the telephone salesperson has done their job, answered all the questions, addressed elements of risk, talked to members of the buying committee, and uncovered all need requirements, and has generated sufficient interest — why not move forward?

Some customers will say, "I need time to think about it" and if so, time is built in for them to do so. But others will be relieved to be done with it, will be impressed by the thoroughness of the salesperson's approach and consultations, and agree, "I don't have any reason we shouldn't move forward." The deal is done. Remember, earlier we said our biggest competitor is probably "do nothing." Use the timeline process to battle "do nothing," that big ugly ogre, the destroyer of deals.

Chapter 9
Building Customer Relationships Over the Phone

Soon after the first dealer exchange in the fall of 2005, I got a call from a dealer requesting scripts. He was hiring a new ISR and he wanted to give this person the script. What should they say over the phone to close sales? I told the dealer ISRs don't use scripts; their calls are open dialogue. The customer's needs are too dynamic and relationship building is too central to be scripted.

"I can provide you with some Call Outlines," I said. "Call Outlines have a suggested call opening, open- and closed-ended questions, business proposal, close and next steps."

"But I don't think my guy will know how to use a Call Outline," he said. "Can you tell him how to do it?"

"Sure, I'd be happy to," I responded. "Why don't I make up a few Call Outlines and email them to you. Give them to your guy, and have him call me. We'll role play how to use them." And as I hung up the phone, I knew this newly minted ISR needed more than a couple of Call Outlines and a conversation with me. He needed training.

Over the years, I have seen a far greater variance in salesperson performance among telephone salespeople than field salespeople. The field salesperson gets substantial credit just for showing up; the telephone salesperson with bad technique is penalized for showing up. The telephone salesperson just interrupted the customer's day and offered nothing of value. The customer now thinks less of the selling organization than before the telephone salesperson picked up the phone.

Technique is critically important. Some telephone salespeople come into the job scared, afraid of the phone. This is called "phone reluctance" and is common. When they realize that with good technique they can make calls customers enjoy taking, and will look forward to their next call, they are relieved. When they realize they can increase their sales participation and closing percentage with good technique, they are impressed. When they realize good technique will potentially raise their salary and/or commission, they are evangelized, and will preach the telephone selling gospel to the next telephone salesperson hired.

Good telephone sales technique is not intuitive. Think about what you normally do when you meet a person for the first time in a business setting face-to-face. Don't you engage in a little small talk first, to break the ice? Think of the last time you met someone on a personal basis for the first time. Isn't it about the same — comments on the weather, whatever? Something to get the conversation going.

On the phone calling business-to-business, this kind of false scene setting is irritating. After all, you have just interrupted the customer's day. It is of no value to engage in idle chit-chat with someone they've never met in person and who obviously is just trying to sell something. In fact, during the idle chit-chat, the customer is thinking about how much they hate these kinds of calls and trying to find a convenient entry point to politely, or not so politely, get rid of this person. In person, it's personal first, business second. On the phone, you must do business first and quickly answer the question, "Why should I talk to you?"

Once you have made the rotation from business issue, to the customer's business, to them personally, the telephone salesperson can be personal. Subsequent calls, after the relationship has been established, revert to the same pattern as field sales — personal first, then business. But not the first call or two.

The second ISR I shadowed at a Cat dealer was in northern Canada. He was a skilled mechanic who always impressed local management by his ability to talk to a customer who stopped by the shop. I landed in Montreal and drove northward with Yannick, his manager. We chatted along the way about the difficulty of serving a multilingual area (French and English), the challenges of serving a customer base scattered throughout a wide geography, and how hard it was to contact their logging customers who would disappear into the bush for days at a time, far out of the reach of the closest cell phone tower. I also was introduced to sugar pie, a delicacy in that part of the world, having over a piece a day. I was so impressed I went on the Internet when I got home and downloaded the recipe.

The night before I met their ISR, we had dinner with their senior management, a fine meal. I appreciated immediately the culinary heritage that came over from France. After dinner, they asked me if I wanted to see the city and I enthusiastically said yes. I remember we toured the shops, decorated for Christmas, and they showed me the famous forts in town. Unfortunately, I had forgotten how cold it can be in Canada in the wintertime, and I wore my dress shoes. (Consultants are always taught to dress one notch above the customer, out of respect). Needless to say my feet were frozen, or at least they felt that way, by the end of the tour. But I was duly impressed with the history of the place, the kindness of the Canadian citizens, especially when you tried a few words of halting French, and the professionalism of the dealer.

Steve, a mechanic-turned-ISR, worked out of a branch location located on the edge of Quebec City. The dealership was industrial functional, and he sat at a desk not far from the parts counter at the front of the store, and close to the door that led to the shop. The ISR obviously was great friends with the mechanics. As they passed by his desk, they exchanged pleasantries, few of which I understood because they were in French. He wore the same uniform as the mechanics and had a list of customers on an Excel worksheet. He began with the top of the alphabet and worked his way down.

He told me about his job and how much he liked helping customers diagnose and fix problems with their equipment. Many of his customers, he explained, were "do-it-myself" customers or customers who do their own repairs, but look to the Cat dealer to supply parts and maintenance supplies. They appreciated his technical knowledge, and he told me about customers who would hold the phone close to equipment with issues, hoping he could diagnose the problem just by the sound.

He was down about to the "F's" on this pass through his spreadsheet of some 2,000 names. He pointed out a few, told me about their businesses and what they owned and then it was time to call. He hesitated a long time, like he was gathering the courage to dial, and as he began to dial I noticed that his hand shook.

The customer answered and the conversation started with hesitations and halts. I was focusing on tone of voice because I didn't understand French, but within a minute the conversation loosened up considerably. Within another minute, after some fast dialogue back and forth, the ISR was looking things up in the business system. He pulled up a diagram of a part and was swiftly describing it to the customer. His hands moved across the screen, they shared laughter. The ISR moved to a note pad, quickly writing down part numbers and what looked like an address, in French of course.

When he hung up the phone, we debriefed. The customer had a problem with a cylinder on a backhoe and needed some parts to fix it. He got an order. I asked him why he was so nervous at the beginning of the call, and why he was so hesitant. He told me that he hated intruding on the customer. They were probably doing something else, and why would they want to talk to him?

I remarked that he had just helped the customer, but he said most of the time they don't need anything. Prior to becoming a telephone sales representative — an ISR — he had been a mechanic for four years and on the parts counter for four years. The first call to the customer was easy. He introduced himself, told the customer he could be a resource, and they exchanged a little bit of information. It was all the subsequent calls where he felt he had little to offer unless the customer had a problem that posed a real challenge to him.

On the drive back to Montreal, Yannick and I worked on a cross- and up-selling matrix for his parts counter advisors who took inbound calls from customers. We talked about the ISR program, and his goal to grow the initiative. Once back in Montreal, I shadowed his other representative, Kimberly, and heard about the same thing I did up in Quebec City — a talented representative who needed guidance on how to make subsequent calls into a database. That evening I went to dinner with their trainer and discussed how we could fill this gap. How we could give their telephone representatives the confidence to open every call, and provide value so customers would welcome this contact. They needed telephone sales training.

But how to serve ISRs scattered across the globe, in small pockets of one or two for the most part? I called Mark when I returned. Earlier I proposed taking our material, customizing everything for Caterpillar, and putting it online. Mark replied that too many dealers had poor Internet connections, especially overseas and in remote locations. I called up my friend Rocky White down at National Seminars Group and asked him what they'd suggest for a training product in these conditions. He sent me over to their product department, and they recommended a series of CDs that could be played either in something like a boom box or in the CD drive of a computer. Almost everyone had access to one or the other.

I proposed this to Mark and gave him a budget. After the back and forth of a typical sales cycle, the budget was approved and we began working on a CD and book series called "Building Customer Relationships Over the Phone." He provided me access to product experts and I traveled the hallways of the marketing areas meeting with product groups, accumulating brochures and technical bulletins. I created three customers, a well-driller, a small contractor, and a small excavation company, which were "do-it-myself," "work-with-me" and "do-it-for-me" customers respectively.

The "do-it-myself" well driller did all their own maintenance and owned competitive equipment; the "work-with-me" customer did some of their own maintenance, and the dealer did some; the "do-it-for-me" excavation company had the dealer do the maintenance. The final course consisted of eight one-hour modules and three modules for the sales manager to teach them how to coach telephone salespeople.

Soon our office was full of plastic clam shells, sleeves for each of the CDs, and a place for a text book. Neal Stromer, our fulfillment and accounting person, became an expert in bundling each of them up and sending them out. He also became an expert in shipping via UPS overseas, which because of customs regulations and the required commercial invoicing, was quite a trick. But soon Neal was sending out dozens across the globe, and translating into Portuguese, Spanish, French, and Mandarin, as dealers began to hire — slowly, very slowly — one ISR at a time.

Chapter 10
DESIGN: Compelling Reason to Call

You are at home in the wintertime, resting after dinner, when you notice the house is chilly. When you trek over to the thermostat, you notice you have it set at 70-F (21-C) and the room is 60-F (15-C). You go to the basement and your old, reliable furnace is silent. You click a few switches, perhaps mutter under your breath, and then pull out your cell phone and call the number on the sticker plastered helpfully on the side of your furnace by the last person who came over for service. You are interested in talking to your service company.

It's a few hours later, the furnace is humming along, the repair wasn't costly, and you are binge watching a favorite series of yours and the phone rings. It's your insurance agent. It's the anniversary of your life insurance policy, and you are eligible for additional insurance without a physical. You are not interested in talking to your insurance agent right away, because he or she just interrupted your laser focus on the fifth episode of the second season.

On the inbound call to customer service, the customer has an interest, or they wouldn't have picked up the phone and gave the selling organization a call. In field sales, being face-to-face generates interest. As mentioned earlier, a field salesperson gets a lot of credit just for showing up. The telephone salesperson must generate interest on every call. Because the brain tends to want to keep doing what it is doing, sufficient interest must be generated to prod the customer into stopping what they were doing before the phone rang and talk to the telephone salesperson. On top of that, a large portion of the human brain is dedicated to processing visual images, and that part of the customer's brain is still doing this task when they say hello. Therefore, the beginning of the call must be compelling for the customer, it must generate interest.

What generates interest? Something immediately relevant to the customer that snaps them out of the trance of what they were doing the moment before the call. "The last time we talked, you told me you were working on the Barker project. How is it going?" "I understand you were assigned to wring out 25% of your inventory investment." "You asked me to give you a call if we had a special or promotion which could save you money." "Your insurance policy will expire at the end of the month, and we should talk about renewal so you don't miss any coverage." The magic word is you. Something about the customer. Something to make them take immediate notice.

The best compelling reason to call is generated from the customer narrative. What do you do if you don't have a customer narrative because you haven't talked to this customer before, and they are only a suspect? The best thing to do is to call someone else besides the decision maker first. Ask yourself, who can I call within the organization to give me some inside information? You aren't looking for anyone to betray any secrets or tell you anything that is confidential, just some information to make the call with the decision maker immediately relevant. In the Caterpillar example, we called Caterpillar University. Because they were inward facing to their employees, and because Caterpillar itself didn't have any salespeople — salespeople are all dealer employees — Caterpillar University couldn't be a customer of ours. However, they may know who could be a customer of ours and could supply us with enough information to make a decision maker call compelling.

Who might assist you, if you are a telephone sales representative or your salespeople if you are a manager?

Think of who within the prospect's organization might be able to tell you information so the call to the decision maker is not a cold call. For example, I once worked for an organization that made hydraulic pumps for other businesses to incorporate into their equipment. We found out that a good place to call was the quality department. They didn't get many calls, and they understood any engineering and quality challenges their company was having with their existing vendors. Due to the new product introduction process, they also knew of any new products their organization was developing, and who was on the team. This allowed me to identify the engineers or designers who would be decision makers, identify what might be some of their key concerns, and to open the call with something like "I understand you are on the team that designed the new XYZ assembly. As part of this assembly, you'll need hydraulic pumps that can perform over 10,000 mean cycles between failure in ambient temperatures of -30 C to 80 C." It's hard to ignore this opening if you're an engineer on this project. It generates interest. Whatever your situation is, think of who can help you on the inside to learn how you can ethically warm up the call with the decision maker.

Another key source of information is the gatekeeper. The gatekeeper is the person who answers the phone and is between you and the decision maker. I distinguish between a gatekeeper and a receptionist. The receptionist's job is to route you to the right department or extension, and probably doesn't know much about the prospect company's operations or business issues. The gatekeeper has a variety of tasks for the organization that expose him or her to relevant business issues, and just one of their jobs is answering the phone.

For example, the telephone salesperson could reach the gatekeeper and say, "My name is John Example from ABC Company. We supply hydraulic pumps to leading manufacturers like yourselves. I understand Sara Customer purchases pumps for your organization. Can I ask you a few questions to see if our products are something she should consider?" The gatekeeper may say, "I guess I wouldn't know, you'll need to talk to Sara directly," which suits John Example just fine, because he was calling for Sara anyway.

But the typical response is, "I'll try to help you," because one of the responsibilities of most gatekeepers is to help. If the gatekeeper answers affirmatively, try the business issue questions from DISCOVER and find out what you can to warm up the call. Whether the gatekeeper can help John Example or not, he has distinguished himself from hundreds of other salespeople calling for Sara because he expressed genuine respect for Sara's time. If John Example has a five-minute chat with the gatekeeper, and piques her interest in his product or service by using the process in DISCOVER, Sara's cell phone number could magically appear. Or, Sara, who was not available when John Example originally called, may suddenly be available because he took the time to generate interest. Many times, I've built this rapport with the gatekeeper, and a decision maker who was "not available" when I first called, mysteriously appeared and I was transferred in. They were there all along of course, but the gatekeeper was an expert screener, and when he or she was convinced I added value, I was in.

Outside information can also be used. If you are selling equipment, you can check the Uniform Commercial Code to see if the prospect has recently financed any equipment. If you are selling to contractors, you can check bid reports to see if they have recently landed any work. The selling organization should always consider what public information is available for their telephone salespeople to warm up a prospect call.

Once the initial call is made, the telephone salesperson should find something within the call to put in their narrative which can be used to open the next call. As mentioned, the narrative is the most powerful way to open a call. What is the customer working on? What new projects did they mention? What new customers are they serving? It can also be something personal, if they mentioned in passing their back was hurting, a great way to open the next call is, "Last time we talked, you mentioned your back was hurting. How are you feeling?"

The telephone salesperson should listen carefully for these offhand personal comments a customer may make on a call, "My back was hurting so I decided to stay in the office this week." "My son has a little league tournament so I won't be back until Tuesday." "We are moving to a new office next week so I won't be available until Friday." These are potential compelling reasons to call for the next call.

If the telephone salesperson does not have something from the customer narrative, the next best call opening is from customer service. Has the customer ordered anything since the last time they talked? See how their order went. Have they brought in something for service? Check and see how it went. Do they have a warranty expiring? Let them know. Is an anniversary date coming? Tell them about it. Something from customer service is a good compelling reason to call because it is something relevant.

The third way to open a call to an existing customer is to introduce a special or promotion. Now this is only compelling if the customer has prequalified the customer's interest on the first call. On the first call, the telephone salesperson should ask, "If I see a special or promotion we are having that can save you money based upon what you have told me about your business, do you want me to give you a call?" Almost all customers say yes to this. Why wouldn't they want to save money with something that is relevant to their business? An example of a compelling reason to call is, "You asked me to give you a call if we had a special or promotion that may help your business. We're having a special on the LMNO drive. Can I ask you a few questions to see if this might be a fit?"

A fourth way to open a call to an existing customer is to introduce something new. Now this is only compelling if the customer has prequalified this. The telephone sales rep should ask on the first call, "If I spot something new in our lineup that may save you money or help your business perform better, do you want me to give you a call?" Again, almost every customer says yes. An example of a compelling reason to call is, "You asked me to give you a call if we had something new in our lineup that may save you money, I was looking over my notes, and I realized the PQRS assembly might be something to explore. Can I ask you a few questions to see if this might be a fit?"

As you can see, if the telephone salesperson qualifies "special or promotion" and "something new" with the customer, they will always have a way to open the call with "You said... " "You mentioned..." or "You asked..." This is far better than anything that begins with "I," such as "I was calling to touch base" or "I haven't talked to you in a while. What's up?" Of course, these are just a couple of phrases that don't sound immediately relevant.

Once the telephone salesperson has warmed up the call and generated interest with a compelling reason to call, they can use a secondary compelling reason to call to get down to business. For example, let's say John Example, a telephone salesperson, is calling on a special his selling organization is having on the XYZ pump assembly. He could just call on the special, because he prequalified to call on specials or promotions, as Sara Customer asked him to. But he knows something from the customer narrative is a more compelling reason to call, and from his notes, he sees Sara told him she was taking a vacation to the Caribbean the last time they talked.

He could open with the compelling reason to call: "Sara, the last time we talked, you mentioned you were going to the Caribbean on vacation. How did it go?" After a discussion about the Caribbean, he could bridge to the sales conversation by using the second compelling reason to call: "Sara, you asked me to give you a call if we were having a special or promotion on something that could help your business. We are having a special on the XYZ pump assembly. Can I ask you a few questions to see if this is something you should consider?" When Sara Customer says yes, the telephone salesperson can ask questions from DISCOVER to generate interest in the XYZ pump assembly, and smoothly transition from the personal to business.

Compelling reasons to call should also be used within a sales cycle, and here is where establishing the steps of the sales cycle and a timeline is critically important. For example, Suzy Salesperson sells industrial paint to roll coaters, companies that produce steel-sided buildings. She has called Barry Buyer at Acme Roll Coating and found Acme has a business issue — they have an opportunity to supply a large builder who has asked for a new trendy color, tangerine citrus. Suzy uncovered the following attributes of her industrial paint product are a real benefit to the buyer — color stability between batches, strong resistance to sun fading, and strong adherence to the steel (no cracking, peeling, or delaminating). Suzy proposed the following sales cycle:

Suzy Salesperson: "Barry, if you were to move forward with us, when would you need the tangerine citrus paint to meet your customer's request?"

Barry Buyer: "We'd need to deliver the first batch in six months. We'd need your paint in-house within four months to meet this schedule."

Suzy Salesperson: "Great. If you choose us as your supplier, I'd need about two months to do our testing and analysis, and get the paint delivered to you. Do you think you can make a decision in two months?"

Barry Buyer: "Sure, I can do that."

Suzy Salesperson: "Okay. To make a good decision, my customers typically go through a series of steps. First, I'd like to provide you with color samples and the spectrum analysis for your customer's approval. This way, we can set a color standard and make sure everyone agrees. Next, I'll provide you with a 50-gallon sample for you to test the application process. Finally, once we have agreed on the composition of the final product, I'll provide you with a quotation and review it with you to make sure you don't have any unanswered questions. How does this sound to you?"

Barry Buyer: "Sounds like a good process."

Suzy Salesperson: "Great. Can we move forward with this plan?"

Barry Buyer: "Yes."

Suzy asked the trial close, "How does this sound to you?" She got a positive response, and then closed on the sales process, "Great. Can we move forward with this plan?" Again, she got a "yes." Suzy performed the first step of the process and shipped a color sample and spectrum analysis to the customer. When she called the customer back to assure the sample and analysis met his needs, her compelling reason to call is, "The last time we talked, you asked me to work with you on your exciting tangerine citrus project. You asked me to send you a color sample and spectrum analysis, and I see it arrived Tuesday. What did you think?" Because Suzy created a sales cycle, and the customer agreed, the compelling reasons to call during the sales cycle can be about the customer ("you said, you mentioned, you asked") and not about Suzy or her selling organization. When the sales cycle is about the buyer—their needs and their deadlines—Suzy has an excellent chance of getting a decision and avoiding the stall.

Each step should include a similar compelling reason to call. On the final call, the call to close the sale, Suzy will introduce the quotation. Good form is to email the quotation to the customer when you have them on the phone. Sometimes customers ask for the quotation beforehand, but it should be avoided if possible.

Continuing this example, Suzy could open this final call like this: "Barry, we've been working on your tangerine citrus opportunity, which you said is important to your business. Congratulations again on getting this order! You asked me to prepare a quotation on your paint needs. May I send the quote over to you, and then review it with you to make sure I have answered any questions?" After answering any questions, and overcoming any objections, Suzy should ask for the sale.

The interest Suzy generated in her product was the vision she painted in the customer's mind of the successful realization of this new order for tangerine citrus steel siding. The paint she is providing is simply a means to make this opportunity a customer reality. When the sales cycle is focused on the customer's opportunity, excitement remains, and the telephone salesperson is truly helping the customer to buy. Competitors that stick their nose under the tent during this process and talk about "my paint," will seem obnoxious and barely relevant by comparison. Who wants to talk about someone else's paint? What they want to talk about is the exciting opportunity to meet the customer's order for the trendy tangerine citrus. Does this mean that Suzy can capture the business without dealing with the competitors? Of course not; a good buyer will still go through the required paces. But Suzy can position herself as the last look, as the confidante, consultant, and favorite. That's her job.

Chapter 11
The Second Exchange

The second dealer exchange for Cat dealer ISRs was held May 10 – 11, 2006, in Tucson, Arizona, with five dealers presenting and 31 attendees representing other dealerships. The focus was to continue to socialize the concept among the dealer community and among the Caterpillar employees who worked in marketing. Now managers would begin to establish benchmarks— such as the best business models and hiring, orientation, training, coaching, and managing techniques.

At Tucson, I met Bill Buss in person for the first time. We had talked on the phone, but had never met face-to-face. He brought along one of his ISRs, Chris Huot, to talk to the dealers. Chris was young with a two-year marketing degree. Members of Bill's team looked up to Bill, not only as a manager, but as a general life advisor. I remember Chris asking Bill about how he should handle a minor disagreement with his future wife, and Bill said "Chris, would you rather be happy or right?" Chris nodded after receiving this great wisdom about relationships and marriage. I couldn't help thinking to myself how perceptive it was, given my experiences in life.

Chris was an aggressive, hard-charging salesperson, and during his presentation he said his greatest concern was to make sure he didn't come on too strong to his customers. He wanted to build relationships for the long term, and not just close the sale in front of him that day. With Bill's encouragement, Chris said he joined Toastmasters, and was elected the local chapter's leader in 2006. He said Bill gave his salespeople four training days a month at the time of the exchange, and encouraged shadowing outside field sales representatives. Chris said he tried to converse with 25 to 30 customers per day, and like many of the ISRs, he typically worked an evening a week to catch customers who were busy during the day. Chris reported he had closed individual sales over the phone up to $18,000.

Bill reported during his presentation he currently had 16 ISRs covering thousands of accounts and generated $35 million in sales. The cost of an individual customer contact over the phone was less than 10% the cost of a field sales call — especially given the large distances in the Finning territory near Edmonton, Alberta, Canada. The dealers talked back and forth a great deal on the business model.

Bill said he assigned accounts equal to $30,000 annually to ISRs and larger to field salespeople. Other dealers assigned smaller customers, with a consensus around annual sales of $10,000 or less.

The next presentation was from Craig Putnal. Larry Czernik, an associate of Mark's, recommended that Craig attend to discuss the results of the salesperson profiling. Craig was a senior manager at Caliper Corporation responsible for international and large corporate sales. Craig reported the results of the study conducted by Mark and his team, and discussed the differences between the ideal field salesperson and telephone salesperson profile. The telephone salesperson needed to be able to do a repetitive job, without visual cues. The field salesperson had travel time each day, and this brought more job variety. The telephone salesperson needed to be detail oriented because they typically handled about six to eight times as many accounts as the field salesperson. Both needed empathy, because they needed to relate to the customer and "feel their pain," but not so much empathy they discarded the legitimate needs of the dealer.

As Craig finished his presentation, a dealer on the corner of the large horseshoe-shaped table for the dealers (consultants and Caterpillar people in the back) wanted to get his attention and obviously struggled to remember his name. Finally he blurted out, "Hey Caliper guy!" The room burst into laughter. From then on, Craig Putnal was simply "Caliper Guy."

Bill, responding to a dealer question, reported receiving about 70 resumes for each position he had open. He screened the resumes, leaving about 30 who went on the next step. During the resume screening, he looked for a background that demonstrated the candidate could do a repetitive job, had an interest in sales, and had some mechanical aptitude, such as working on cars or in construction. The 30 who remained were given a telephone interview. The goal of the 10- to 15-minutes telephone interview was to exclude those who obviously couldn't do the job, and the expectation was the candidate would sell the hiring manager on inviting them into a face-to-face interview. About eight out of the 30 would be asked to come into the dealership for a face-to-face interview, which typically lasted an hour. The interview was behavioral based, and designed to determine whether the candidate had demonstrated behaviors in the past that were necessary to be successful in telephone sales.

On average, three to four would go on to the next step which was to shadow an existing ISR. The purpose of this shadow was two-fold, first so the telephone sales candidate could see the job. Some would decide after seeing what was involved to take themselves out of the process. Bill said he would also interview the employee the candidate shadowed. Did the candidate ask good questions? Did they seem interested in the job? Would they fit into the culture? Finally, the best candidate would be selected, references checked, and a hire made.

As a group, the dealers discussed their training process. There was a consensus around a six-week training process, involving product knowledge, sales skills, and shadowing around the dealership to gain application knowledge. Everyone had their ISRs accompany the field salespeople to visit customer sites. Our CD-based training, "Building Customer Relationships Over the Phone," was used to build sales skills.

We also conducted a roundtable on management and telephone salesperson's need for emotional nutrition. The telephone salesperson is typically a new hire, often young, and at times overwhelmed by the product knowledge and sales skills needed to do a good job. This requires the manager to be supportive and more involved than they may be with field salespeople.

Typically, at American Media, a company I worked at previously as the Vice President of Sales and Marketing, I'd ask the salespeople to attend a sales meeting with a reference story ready, one about a customer solving a business issue by using our product or service, and an objection they had recently overcome. These stories can be shared, both for teambuilding and skill building. We recommended recurring product training, just to keep the telephone salespeople sharp, and updates on what is going on in their territory — new projects starting up, new developments, politics, anything that could influence what customers buy and what needs they might have.

The exchange concluded with a discussion on how these managers could sell the ISR concept to senior managers at the dealership. Mark turned to me and asked me to put together a presentation these managers could use to "sell" their dealer management on implementing the ISR concept. I put together a PowerPoint and a facilitator's guide for managers to present the concept to dealer executives.

After the exchange, I met with Mark and other Caterpillar representatives who had attended the event, and I was also asked to update the Implementation Guidebook. The object was to incorporate the best practices captured at the two dealer exchanges, and for me to add in materials from Business Performance Group's experience.

The new Implementation Guidebook would contain chapters on constructing a business model, hiring new telephone sales representatives, orientation from both the dealership and the salesperson perspective, training, coaching, managing, and leading.

As we left Arizona, the number of dealers interested in implementing the concept had doubled from the last dealer exchange eight months before.

Chapter 12
DESIGN: Marketing Meets Sales

Earlier in my career, I was the Director of Sales and Marketing at a seminar company. We did a series of one- and two-day seminars across the country that we marketed by sending out millions of four- or eight-page brochures to our house file and third-party lists we'd rent. We had a seminar called "How to Hire Great Employees!" This was a mediocre performer at best, although the content on behavioral-based interviewing was top notch, the presenter was first rate, and the topic was hot. What to do? We had a meeting and my boss said we should test the title, to see if we couldn't come up with something more engaging, try a different positioning. After a mind-numbing number of titles were thrown up on the white board, someone in our meeting came up with the idea to call the seminar "How to Avoid Hiring Lemons, Nuts, and Flakes!" Wow, show stopper. Provocative. Revolutionary. It just might work.

It did in a very big way. Where we had 25 attendees before, we now had 175. Rooms overflowed; we needed to rent a bigger space. We ran out of workbooks. The interior of these suddenly scarce workbooks was the same, with a different title. Our presenter was the same. The cities were the same. Just the title was different. We also received a letter from the Lemon family asking why we were encouraging people not to hire them and letters from various mental health associations asking us why we were encouraging people not to consider people with mental disabilities—all nuances we hadn't frankly considered. The title was quietly dropped.

Why did one title produce poor results and one title spectacular results? Positioning. The first positioning was the standard "fulfill the need" positioning—come to our seminar and we'll teach you how to hire. Yawn, sorry, dozed off for a second. There are a lot of offerings like this out there. The second positioning was "develop the need," the need to avoid hiring bad employees. Same seminar, different positioning. When you see the brochure "How to Avoid Hiring Lemons, Nuts, and Flakes" as a hiring manager, don't you immediately think back to all the bad hires you've made, how much you invested, how painful it was to let them go? At a gut level, "How to Hire Great Employees!" comes across as I probably know all that stuff, whereas "How to Avoid Hiring Lemons, Nuts, and Flakes" comes across as "wow, I've make a mistake like that. What do they know that I don't know?"

One of the most undervalued but critical considerations in any direct marketing effort like telephone sales is how your telephone sales representatives are positioned with the customer. Many managers don't make this decision, and the reps themselves just adopt a positioning by default. It is far better to think about it, perhaps test a few approaches, and then make sure your telephone sales representatives are adopting the right approach.

Positioning is selecting the most advantageous mental architecture against your competition. Horizontal positioning is determining your entry point in the customer's buying process. Vertical positioning is determining what customer segments a telephone sales representative will go after. Who will they call? For example, if you have a customer database of 1,000 customers or prospects, and you'd like to call them, build a relationship, and pursue additional sales, who do your telephone sales representatives call first? Second? Last? How can you score them based on opportunity?

Vertical positioning, or segmentation, relies on two characteristics of your customers or prospects — their demographics and psychographics. Demographics are descriptors of the businesses you intend to target. For example, how many employees do they have? How many offices? How many installed machines? You probably have data points like this that are important to you. SIC codes are used in the United States as industry demographics.

Psychographics deal with corporate behavior. If you are selling workman's compensation insurance, what is the prospect's or customer's attitude toward safety? If you are selling preventive maintenance services, what is their attitude about service — run until failure, or do they invest in preventive maintenance? Businesses with identical demographics may have quite different corporate cultures, producing quite different psychographics and sales results.

For example, I once managed an outbound telephone selling group that sold training products to corporations, mostly to trainers who conducted face-to-face, facilitated learning sessions. A psychographic data point for me was, "How many subscriptions to Training Magazine does this location have?" Another was, "How many members of the American Society of Training and Development does this location have?" (Now the Association for Talent Development.)

I knew our targeted demographics (medium to large businesses), and scored each with these two data points. We started calling the highest-scoring prospects first. Within their customer base (people who have purchased before), we used both their purchases (past buying behavior) and these two data points (future opportunity) to develop planned annual rates of call (PAR). A company with low sales but large potential opportunity based on psychographics may get as many calls as a company with higher sales but low additional opportunity.

Horizontal positioning is designed to put your competitors in a "mental box." Positions include "develop the need," "fulfill the need," "sell against your competition," "sell on price" or "sell based on urgency." "Develop the need" is helping the customer define their business issue — problem, opportunity, or strategy — in such a way that the selling organization's product or service can be the best solution. For example, if a customer wants to reduce the downtime of their production machinery, the best solution might be the selling organization's preventive maintenance service.

As I indicated earlier, this is usually the best positioning to take if you have a good business relationship with the customer. This positioning facilitates a consultative selling approach. Get in early and help the customer define the problem in terms the selling organization can solve.

"Fulfill the need" assumes the customer already has a need, knows they need to buy something, and the selling organization is here to take care of it. If the telephone sales representative works for a company selling workman's compensation insurance, businesses are required to have it. Therefore, the selling organization is fulfilling the need. In this case, the selling organization may or may not be in a competitive position.

"Selling against the competition" is when your product or service is clearly better than the competition, and any time you are in a bake-off with competitors, you'll win a fair share of the business. This also assumes you don't need to create any needs; the customer already has needs, know they need to buy a solution, and are actively considering alternative vendors.

"Selling on price" is when the telephone salesperson clearly has a lower-priced product or service. For example, I recently switched payroll providers for my company. The telephone salesperson who called me knew they had a price-competitive offering, and it should be sufficient to convince me to switch. There's not much product differentiation. For all the vendors I know, everything is done online, and all the federal and state withholding and reporting requirements must be met and filed. Therefore, price was the major consideration, and the price differentiation had to be sufficient to override the switching hassle of re-entering everyone's payroll information. The salesperson focused on this.

What if the salesperson had adopted one of the previous positions? "Develop the need" would work well for organizations currently doing their own payroll. "Fulfill the need" would work for organizations that have decided to outsource payroll but haven't selected a provider or done a search yet. "Selling against the competition" would probably not work as well, because there is little service differentiation.

This organization selected to start with price to get attention and generate interest, and because most businesses with our longevity probably outsource. If I answered the telephone sales rep's initial question on price, "We do our own payroll," or "We were just considering outsourcing," the positioning of "We are a low-cost provider" is a pretty good place to start the conversation, and a good positioning entry point to generate interest and get the call going.

"Selling based on urgency" is when the telephone salesperson can offer their product or service quicker than the competition. For example, the selling organization may be open 24 hours a day, or offer overnight delivery, or a quick turnaround time. For example, on the consumer side, you see some fast food advertisers focus on "fast delivery." They are not trying to make you hungry. Nor are they comparing their pizza or sandwiches or whatever to the competition's in terms of taste or quality. They have selected a positioning that works for them.

The right positioning decision can make a staggering difference in your success. For example, I have a client who sells a form of employee personality assessment over the telephone. We have two major segments: prospects who have used similar assessments before, and those who have not. For customers who have not used assessments before, we adopted the "develop the need" positioning by focusing on the business issues an assessment can help solve. For prospects who have used similar assessments, we adopted the "fulfill the need" positioning. We didn't need to go all the way up and "develop the need." These businesses already know about employee assessments.

We considered "selling against the competition," but we decided it would be better to position ourselves one position higher. If we were "selling against the competition," we would present how we are different and best. Quite frankly, since our assessment is based on the same psychological model (although it is better and much newer), we didn't think this comparison would be sufficiently appealing.

Our assessment is less expensive, but we decided not to use a price positioning because it makes us seem cheap, and may indicate less value. We decided because our assessment was new, and the competitors had been around for decades, that we could be "not your grandfather's assessment," which was true, since our assessment depends on the computing power of the cloud. We could talk about our competitors as "being good in their day," which is to throw them under a velvet tired bus, and the fact that our assessment is less expensive, "as an extremely affordable solution to your business issue, only $39 per person."

By selecting the positioning, we determined the mental architecture customers will construct piece by piece as the dialogue goes along. Consider, "We offer a cost-effective solution to your business issue" vs. "We're less expensive than assessment 'X,' they are $70 per person and we are only $39." And consider "We are not your grandfather's assessment. Our assessment was never paper-based; our assessment was born online and designed for millennials, who are now more than half of today's workforce."

Assessment 'X' was good in its day," vs. "Our assessment is better than 'X' because it uses a complex evaluation algorithm which cannot be done on paper." If you are talking to a business manager, which argument provides motivation to change, momentum to move to something new? "A little cheaper using a more complex algorithm," or "A new, inexpensive assessment designed for today's workforce. What you are using now is your grandfather's assessment, good in its day."

We found that going against entrenched competitors directly on product didn't give customers enough of a reason to change vendors. Going directly against price, because we are less expensive — comparing our price "A" against our competitor's price "B" — didn't give customers enough of an incentive to change vendors. But positioning ourselves as "not your grandfather's assessment" (we are new) and "extremely affordable" (because it is inexpensive) we are the perfect cost-effective assessment to use with the millennials — the new generation which is over half of the workforce. Nuances matter. Perception is reality, and positioning drives perception.

What if a product or service is a better value than the competition? The investment required (the price) is higher as well. What positioning should the selling organization adopt? This selling organization can adopt any of the positions — "develop the need," "fulfill the need," "sell against their competition," "sell on price" or "sell based on urgency." It may even have different positions for different segments. The goal of the salesperson is to demonstrate the product or service meets more needs than the competition, and is well worth the additional investment. When you offer a product or service of higher value, it opens up more positions you can take in the marketplace.

For example, say we are planning to launch a service which destroys confidential documents for businesses. This is appealing for anyone who routinely produces and disseminates paper copies of information that must be protected. We are a local outfit, and national chains are competitors of ours. As we sit around the kitchen table, we brainstorm ways of making our service stand out, deciding we can also destroy old computer hard drives to protect information. We also decide to partner with your brother-in-law who is a cyber security expert to provide an "independent confidentiality audit," which will provide advice to the customer's information technology folks on how they can further protect document security.

Our customers can tell their clients they are going the extra mile to be secure. We'll also recycle the paperwork so we can provide our customers with a "thank you for being green" sticker. What else, we ponder, can we do to make ourselves stand out? We decide we can offer a "document retention" service. We can truck your confidential documents in a locked bin to our guarded storage facility, and destroy them after a certain period when any legal timeframes have passed.

We buy a truck with a big paper grinder in it, and we'll go from customer to customer carrying out their bins of confidential documents and grind them to bits right by their front door. We also have a locked area to transport storage documents on the truck, and the brother-in-law is eager to get started. We named the company "Doc-U-Shield."

Now we must sell our service. We hire a great sales manager, and around the kitchen table again, with our new storage facility nearing completion and our shiny truck ready to hit the road, we decide how to sell this service. First, we procure a list of the businesses within a 50-mile radius of our facility which may have confidential documents in sufficient quantity to warrant our service. Next, we create a flier, killer website, and social media pages. We hire a telephone salesperson to follow up on leads and make cold calls. Our goal too is that they build relationships with customers to cross- and up-sell additional services from our portfolio.

What positioning should we take?

"Develop the Need": We are your confidentiality partner.

"Fulfill the Need": We can protect all your confidential documents, from printer to recycling.

"Sell Against the Competition": We are your trusted and local document security provider.

"Sell on Price": We are the best value in document security.

"Sell Based on Urgency": No time to worry about the security of your documents? Let us help.

We should probably test our approach and see what works best. We should also look at our vertical segments. Perhaps law firms and medical clinics would find "confidentiality partner" appealing. Maybe "trusted and local" would be best for businesses that are owned locally and may be wary of our national competitors, and "best value" would work well for situations where we have an entrenched competitor. "No time" might be the best for fast growing companies where the staff is likely to be stretched. "We can protect your confidential documents, from printer to recycling" may be the best positioning when none of these other positions fit. The sales manager should test all the positions to see what works best to whom.

A properly trained telephone sales representative should be comfortable switching positions on the call, based on the initial answers to their probing questions. In my example of the payroll provider, if they are cold calling a customer and find out they do their own payroll, they can switch from selling on price to developing the need. If the initial questioning determines the customer knows they need to outsource, but haven't done anything about it yet, they can switch to fulfill the need. And if the customer is just putting together a request for proposal to solicit payroll service vendors, they can sell against the competition. If the customer's accountant just left, they can switch to urgency by asserting they can get them up and going on their payroll system quickly. I'm here to help!

The initial positioning is the sales manager's guidance as to what will generate the best initial interest. Once the phone call is underway, the telephone sales representative should be trained to flex their positioning to suit each potential customer. This is one of the many reasons telephone sales representatives are deployed.

Positioning drives the questions your telephone salesperson asks, the compelling reason to call, the potential steps in the sales process and closing statement. All positioning information can be gathered into a Call Outline. A Call Outline is not a script. Telephone selling is open-dialogue, and unlike its rougher and less sophisticated nephew telemarketing, each conversation is unique. But a Call Outline gives the telephone sales representative guidance and assures the manager the best positioning is followed. For the rep, it provides a pathway so they can focus on listening, not on what they will say next.

By making the outbound call, the telephone salesperson initiates the conversation, therefore they have the obligation to carry the phone call and provide the direction. Too often, the salesperson is so nervous about this responsibility, they focus solely on what they will ask next — not the nuances of the answers they are given. For example, a telephone salesperson may be talking to a customer and ask the closed-ended question, "When is your current janitorial contract due for renewal?" The customer answers, "Well, I was just checking last week, but I got interrupted and had to take time off to take care of my mom. Let me pull up that contract... okay... here it is. It expires on December 10th." The telephone sales representative asked the question and was looking for a date. While the customer was looking up the date, the telephone rep was thinking to themselves, "What do I ask next?" All they heard was "December 10th," which was the direct answer to their question. The telephone sales rep completely missed the background information, "I got interrupted and had to take time off to take care of my mom." Why is this valuable? A great way to start the next call would be to use the compelling reason to call "Last time we talked, you mentioned you needed to take time off to take care of your mom. How is she doing?"

If the representative has a Call Outline, all they do is look down and the next question is right there. They can be carefully listening. They'll catch this very important information about mom. Mom matters.

Chapter 13
Steve Jobs Changes Everything

In June of 2006, Bill Buss invited Mark and me to Edmonton to pilot High-Impact Telephone Sales for his ISR team. Mark was joined by his boss, Bob Morrison, and teammate, Larry Czernik. As luck would have it, the Edmonton Oilers hockey team was in the Stanley Cup finals against an American club. Canadians are very passionate about their hockey. One night during our stay, we went out to a restaurant with an attached bar packed with hockey fans cheering the Oilers. Larry, who never met a stranger in his life, thought this was a good time to strike up a conversation and to let people know he was from the United States, the home of the opposing team. Mark and I quickly caucused and discussed if we needed to make a quick exit, but everything remained civil, eh.

I had fifteen ISRs in the class with Bill Buss, Mark, Bob, and Larry sitting in the back of the room. At the end of the very productive session, we debriefed and decided to add some material to the risk evaluation area of the course to highlight the benefit of preventive maintenance. Bill pointed out that 75% to 80% of the dealer's service work was due to breakdowns, not preventive maintenance or scheduled component replacement. The risk to the customer is downtime, and scheduled replacement has huge benefits for both the customer and the dealer.

For the first time, Bill floated the idea of an ISR Boot Camp where the new telephone sales representative would be immersed in training for the job with this selling course being first, and then time on the phone with a coach after. We would end up testing this idea three times, and then rolling out the initiative in a big way in 2011.

Within the next year, business-to-business telephone selling would change dramatically when Steve Jobs' Apple Computer rolled out the iPhone in late June 2007. Prior to this, almost everyone in business had a cell phone, but now everyone had a computer in their pocket. For ISRs, this meant customers could take pictures of leaks, take a video of smoke that wasn't the right color, and send audio of a clunking sound in a compartment that just didn't seem right. The ISR could send quotes and marketing collateral that could be viewed in an instant by a customer or prospect with a smart phone. Purchase orders could be electronically signed, and all this could be done customer-to-customer without a gatekeeper in between. Of course, just as in the world before

June 29, 2007, you had to have a relationship with the customer or prospect before you'd get their smart phone number, and a good enough relationship that they'd answer their phone, but then we've already talked about how to build a relationship.

The nuances of the release of the iPhone, and later its competitors, were far reaching. The next time you go to a public gathering such as a sports show or concert, take a look around as people are waiting for the event to start. Isn't a good share of the crowd looking at their phones? They are probably checking texts, maybe a few tweets, email, social media, voicemails, the weather, and maybe talking to someone. These vehicles are all in the telephone sales representative's domain. Of course, we didn't realize at the time, but this transformation would lead to a burst of hiring activity at Cat dealers after the great recession had passed.

Today, marketing can automate texts and emails to assist the sales effort. Perhaps a prospect has told the telephone sales representative, "I'm interested, but not now. Call me back in six months and we'll talk about it." How can the selling organization keep this prospect warm? Well, the telephone sales representative can call back, and should (at perhaps three months) to continue building the relationship, but more frequently may be considered irritating. Personalized trigger emails and text messages can help. Monthly, the marketing automation system can send out items such as case studies of successful users of the product or service, and promotions and offerings tailored to what is a benefit to the customer.

If the telephone sales representative has done his or her job, they ought to have documented in their notes the benefits they have prequalified. For example, if the email begins, "Last time we talked, you mentioned you would consider installing new lighting in your production area in five months. What was important to you was cost savings, less eye strain for your workers, and less maintenance. We have just completed a case study on a customer's cost savings, and you asked me to forward you any new information which would be helpful. You asked me to give you a call back in two months; I look forward to our conversation." When the prospect gets this email, they'll see the magic word "you" with their hot buttons — cost savings, less eye strain, and less maintenance — and this will keep them warm. If their timetable changes, which salesman will they call?

Another helpful tactic is to remind the telephone sales representative to find out what the initiative is called within the selling organization. As of this writing, many companies in our database have "Plan 2020" or something similar, indicating initiatives around the year 2020 and playing off perfect vision being 20/20. If the representative in the previous example knew this lighting initiative was part of "Vision 2020," this would make a great subject heading for this email: "Your Vision 2020 Initiative."

Almost every business names its initiatives. They have inside slang, abbreviations, three-letter acronyms, or shorthand. Ask! When the salesperson is an insider, the sale is significantly easier. The salesperson is then a consultant, helping the buyer on the "Vision 2020" initiative, not a vendor flogging the latest product that hit the selling organization's shelves, desperately trying to generate interest by feature spraying, hoping something will stick.

We are working with telephone sales representatives who have a substantial number of customers who they communicate with almost exclusively via text message with the occasional email — at the customer's request. These representatives remember our guidance that you can't have a business relationship unless you talk with a customer or prospect at least quarterly, but these conversations are then rich and often lengthy, allowing time to catch up regarding opportunities and strategies. Information transfer has occurred via text or email. What remains is hugely productive dialogue — a great business conversation.

Today, sales conversations that focus on data seem boring and slow. With terabytes of information at everyone's fingertips on the computer they carry in their pocket, they don't need a human relaying it. We comprehend much faster than we talk. In today's fast-paced world, people would rather look it up and read it or see it on video than to listen.

Where will this all go? Business-to-business data continues to be pushed out of the conversation, relegated to the digital: web, text, email, and perhaps the representative's customer-only social media site. What remains is analog. Human beings don't have digital minds. Human beings create analogies, we have flights of fancy, we hope and dream, we struggle to convert the projects that end up on desks into "to do" lists. This is the meaningful stuff of business opportunities and strategies.

It is extremely difficult to uncover opportunities and strategies with a customer survey. Perhaps some problems will pop up in a survey. But the money is usually in the opportunity or strategy, where the customer really doesn't have a vendor yet, because the business issue is undefined, undocumented, or unexplored. Don't we want our telephone sales representatives to have crucial conversations on how they can help their customers get that huge capital investment project done — the one the CEO just dumped on their desk? Use your electronic resources to communicate data. Use your humans to have impactful conversations.

Data is a commodity. Human insight is not. What are your customer's core interests? Do your sales representatives know? And if they don't, who in your organization will?

Chapter 14
DEMONSTRATE: The Sales Conversation

Before I started Business Performance Group, I was the Vice President of Sales and Marketing at American Media, which was, at the time, the world's largest producer of video training products. If you have ever sat through an orientation program on avoiding sexual harassment or attended a facilitated session on building great teams, or how to create a diverse workforce, you have probably watched a video from this industry.

When I arrived, I had an extremely young workforce; many in the sales group were on their first or second jobs, many fresh out of college. As we grew, we had a field sales force of three, a telephone salesforce of 21 and an inbound call center of 12. Our target audience was the corporate trainer or human resources professional at any company with over 100 employees. At the time, I estimated this audience was about 54,000 in the United States, scattered hither and yon across corporate America. We had international distributors who took care of business outside of the U.S., and a domestic distributor network, all managed by another sales group, which consisted of four people.

My boss explained to me when I started that our products resembled a three-act Shakespeare play, with an introduction to set the characters, the struggle and conflict, and finally the resolution. Before purchasing, buyers would preview the product by watching a physical preview the company sent out. Later, as technology evolved, the previews were done online. Because of this, our telephone sales representatives had extremely nuanced conversations. Prior to making up their mind, the customer would watch the product. There were no hidden features, no submerged benefits to bring forward. They either liked it or not. Period.

So how to sell a product someone either liked or didn't? How can we influence the buying decision when it was based almost entirely on personal preference? Well, we can help create the preference before they see the product. We could find out what their business issue is and find out what are they trying to change by using it in their training sessions. We could position our product as the solution before they watched it. Watching it would confirm our positioning. We human beings have confirmation bias; we want new facts to support what we already believe.

For example: "You have a problem with sexual harassment. What aspect? Very interesting, so you are mainly interested in compliance training to avoid legal problems. Tell me about your work environment."

"You have a new opportunity which requires you to form cross-discipline teams? You want your teams to work better together. Okay, tell me more about that. What departments are on the team?"

"Your CEO has a strategy to make your organization number one in customer service in your industry within three years. He thinks training all the front-line people in customer service and promoting a diverse workforce will make all the difference in the world. Wow, tell me about it. If you could wave your magic wand, what in your culture would you change?"

The job of our telephone salesperson was to help the customer take the leap from their business issue to our generic off-the-shelf product against all the other generic-off-the-shelf products available. Of course, when our videos were created, our production department had to pick an office or other location to stage the drama, and few customers would have this identical setup. The telephone salesperson's job was to sell the dream and paint the vivid picture of our product hitting the nail on the head. Their job was to smoke out objections in advance and minimize their impact—a job of pure salesmanship, one requiring a brilliant sales conversation.

Hardly anything in business is more mentally taxing than conducting a good sales conversation. It's like playing tennis with a budding novice and the salesperson's job is to return softly each volley and each serve gently to the customer to keep the game going. Some business issues, mainly problems, are straightforward enough—the customer knows what they need to buy. Match point. But opportunities and strategies are often still vague and ill defined. As the customer tries to work out if they should buy something, how they should buy and when, the balls are hit all over the court. The salesperson needs to be nimble, quick on their feet, and a pro.

A good telephone sales conversation is where the salesperson talks 40% of the time and the customer 60%. Customers reveal their needs, their perceptions of risk, their timelines, and who will impact their buying decision when they are talking. When the salesperson is talking, they need to be positioning their product or service as a solution, not feature spraying or offering non-relevant data. If I could give every telephone salesperson calling business-to-business one injection, I'd give them an inoculation of business curiosity. What makes this customer tick? What is the definition of their problem, opportunity, or strategy?

It's like the old tale of blind people describing the elephant, one at its ear, one at its trunk, one at its hind leg, and one at its tail. All individuals would have a different impression of what an elephant is. The telephone representative must have sufficient business curiosity to know the whole elephant; they need to completely understand the business issue to adequately position the selling organization's product or service as the solution.

Many telephone representatives feel if they talk enough, if they are eloquent enough, and if they are persuasive enough, they'll succeed. Here is a little secret of selling business-to-business, it's not that easy. You may be able to occasionally sell ice to Eskimos on the consumer side where the buying committee consists of one or possibly two people and the risks are generally quantifiable. But in business-to-business, someone the salesperson doesn't talk to will influence the buying decision.

Risk is usually more complex and nuanced and it's usually not the buyer's money. The buyer is making a decision which his or her organization or boss will judge as good or bad. Their job performance will be evaluated based on the quality of the decision. On the consumer side, it's the customer's money, use it as you wish, take a lark, buy that new car, and take a fling on the brand-new house. In business, it's the buyer's job, their security, and their career. In business-to-business, be curious. Peel that onion of a business issue.

Reflection

I recommend the telephone sales representative have a good call outline, and the positioning should be determined by marketing or management in consultation with the sales team. As open-ended questions are asked, the customer will pull off the first layer of the business issue. A good next step is to consider reflecting back what the customer just said to peel off the next layer of the business issue. Consider this case study from one of our telephone sales clients who sells supplies to businesses that own and operate car washes:

Salesperson — *Compelling Reason to Call / Open-Ended Question:* "Sara, the last time we talked, you mentioned your organization was purchasing seven new car washes in the valley and hoped to close by this month. How is the acquisition coming along?"

Customer — *Business Issue Layer One:* "Fine, I guess. But I'm not getting any more help. I've got to buy all the supplies and arrange all the maintenance on these facilities, in addition to our other twenty."

Salesperson — *Reflection:* "Sounds like a big job."

Customer — *Business Issue Layer Two:* "It is. The former owner used completely different vendors. Some contracts run for another two years. Others are buy-as-you-go. You can't believe how many people I have calling me and stopping by. Everyone's nervous they will be losing our business."

Salesperson — *Reflection:* "So on top of your regular job — and I know you were already busy — you have to wrestle with incorporating a whole new team."

Customer — *Business Issue Layer Three:* "Absolutely. For example, the vendor they had for detergent, polish, rinse — you know the consumables — this is his only account in the county. Now, how he got in there I'll never know."

Salesperson — *Closed-Ended Question:* "Would it be helpful for you to consolidate your workload, to do what you were doing before only on a larger scale?"

Customer: "That would be helpful."

Salesperson: "Okay. <pauses> I have an idea. <benefit statement> You said you'd like to consolidate. <business proposal> I could have Jim, our route guy who services your account now, stop by all seven of your new car washes and do an inventory of the consumables. I could provide you a plan of how we could begin servicing these seven new facilities. You'd have just one vendor, you already know about our quality and service and how Jim services your facilities. We could do an audit for you, and then you could make a good decision on how to move forward. <trial close> How does that sound?"

Customer: "You'd be willing to do that?"

Salesperson: "Of course. I want to be your business partner, and I want to be part of the solution and not the problem. Jim has done this for me before. <close> May I set this up for you?"

Customer: "Sure, send me your list when you are done."

Salesperson: "I'll do that. <pause> Sara, what else is important to you as you consider consolidating vendors?"

Customer: "We need to save money on everything because of our larger scale. Our owners paid a premium for these new sites because they felt they could wring out cost savings across the network."

Salesperson: "So a cost-effective bundle is important. <pause>

Anything else?"

Customer: "We have to keep up our quality. Customers have a lot of choices out there."

Salesperson: "Okay quality. <pause> We'll get right on this and I'll give you a call back when we've completed the inventory."

What if our car wash supply salesperson had just started out swinging for the fences to try to capture the new business without probing for the business issues? Our salesperson would be part of the problem (too many vendors pounding on this customer), not part of the solution (simplifying and consolidating the buying process). Once the solution to this business issue was agreed upon (the field audit), the salesperson uncovered other needs.

When I learned how to land a small airplane, my instructor taught me that you get the airplane about three feet off the ground and then just let it settle in; don't fly the plane into the ground because your passengers will get cranky and expensive machinery will get damaged. Manage the sales conversation the same way; keep your product off the table until the business issue is settled.

Restatement

Another good technique is to use the benefit statements uncovered during the needs analysis to present your product. Revisiting the case study of the telephone salesperson who sells supplies to car washes, when the audit is complete and he calls the customer to discuss, he has three benefits he has uncovered: she wants to consolidate vendors, she wants a price reduction for the larger volumes, she wants superior quality which keeps them successful in the marketplace. Let's listen in on the next conversation:

Salesperson: "Sara, <compelling reason to call> you asked me to give you a call back when we've completed the audit. Can I email it to you now and then review it with you to make sure I've answered any questions?"

Customer: "Sure, send it over. <pauses> I got it. <pauses> Interesting."

Salesperson: "You've got probably three months of inventory in the system, but it is not uniform. Several stores will run out in a couple of weeks, and others have six months of supply."

Customer: "What a mess..."

Salesperson: "Sara, <benefit restatement> you told me consolidating vendors was important to you. You also told me you needed to save money by consolidating while keeping your quality up. I also sent you a quotation for us to take over the consumables at your new facilities. We can offer a 10% discount because of the volume, and we'll provide the same quality products which have kept you in your leadership position. I also am proposing wringing over $20,000 out of your supply inventory, by servicing your new facilities weekly, just-in-time."

By restating the benefits, this salesperson kept the presentation about the customer, not about them.

Refuel

The telephone salesperson should always have their ears open for any additional steps they need to add to the selling cycle. What possible steps might the salesperson in our car wash supplies example be ready to add? There may be managers at the new facilities he should consult. Perhaps the route manager should drop off samples of their products for these individuals to test. No sales cycle is stagnant. It is dynamic, and the salesperson should always be sensitive to additional members of the buying committee joining the process, along with their needs and risks.

Reference Stories

I have done many platform speeches over the years and taught numerous sessions of our courses, and when I gaze into the crowd, I notice people always smile when you tell them a story. Content may be king, but the story is engaging entertainment. Since time eternal we have used stories to illustrate, stories to inform and stories to entertain. The telephone sales equivalent is called a reference story, a brief tale of another customer solving a business issue using the selling organization's product or service. The reference story includes a brief description of the business the selling organization helped, their business issue (problem, opportunity or strategy), why the problem happened, what your customer wanted to achieve, what your product or service provided, and the end result.

"I have another customer who owns a chain of six car washes. They recently purchased another four washes in Ida Grove, and were struggling with integrating their supply chains. My contact in corporate purchasing wanted to get a handle on her inventory, and to figure out a way to simply their purchasing process since they had almost doubled in size. I arranged to have one of our route managers visit the new facilities free of charge. He provided a complete report of inventory and how purchasing could be centralized. This allowed my contact to increase efficiency and reduce her workload back to what she had before, a huge relief for her."

How many good reference stories does a telephone salesperson need?

Not many, and they shouldn't sound scripted. They are stories after all. Managers can help cultivate a good storytelling culture by using sales meetings to swap stories and by requiring that everyone share. If you need to illustrate you provide good customer service — serve the story of the time Betty delighted a customer who wasn't expecting an answer until Tuesday. If you need to illustrate your product works good under water, splash out the scuba diving story that happened to Joe. If you need to show you can deliver in a hurry, wheel out the story of Susie biking around the traffic jam. Customers love a good story—short and to the point.

I began this chapter by mentioning American Media and the job of selling training videos over the phone, an exercise in pure selling. The job of the salesperson was to pre-set the customer's perception of the product before they watched it and to position their product as the solution. This is possible if the telephone salesperson understands the real business issue, knowing enough about their product to position it as the solution.

As I mentioned, human beings have what is called confirmation bias, which means we use new information we acquire to confirm what we already believe. Once we as humans have made up our mind, it is very hard to get us to change. The job of the salesperson at American Media was to paint the picture of their video as a great fit before the customer watched it. Watching it only confirmed this belief.

The successful telephone salesperson uses his or her relationship to get to the opportunity first, uses their understanding of the business issue to position their product or service first, uses stories of how others have solved the same issue first, and therefore positively assures all the selling organization's competitors that follow in his or her wake will be competing not only against selling their solution, but the customer's engrained confirmation bias.

Oh, and I have a large original manufacturing customer (OEM) that was struggling with coverage. They historically deployed a field salesforce, but thousands of smaller customers were too expensive to cover face-to-face. They wanted an effective, relationship-building coverage option with the benefits of personal selling, but not the cost. We worked with them to broaden a telephone selling initiative they had within their dealer network to a global solution. Today these inside sales representatives cover hundreds of thousands of accounts, generating close to a billion dollars in sales. A win for the company, its dealers, customers, and shareholders.

I hope you smiled when you read that story.

Chapter 15
International Flavors

Tom had a wedding to attend. This was a problem, because I needed him to be in Shanghai a short time after the ceremony and he had a trip across the Pacific to make in between. Looking at the available flights, I realized that if he left the wedding reception and went directly to the St. Louis airport, we could get him to Los Angeles and then on a red-eye to Tokyo and then over to Shanghai. He'd arrive at the hotel about 2 a.m. I adjusted the agenda so he didn't have to speak until the afternoon.

Before I left for China, I asked him to sleep in the morning he arrived. We agreed he'd be at the dealer exchange by 10:30, and he'd take a cab over to the facility. Tom was the central part of the exchange, because he managed the telephone selling operation at the dealership in Birmingham, Alabama, and was an engaging speaker, with a comforting southern drawl. Dealers learn from dealers, and once he began talking dollars and Yuan (the Chinese currency), the interest level would skyrocket.

The morning of the exchange I woke up, and before breakfast, eagerly went to the front desk just to make sure Tom had checked in at 2 a.m. and that everything was okay. The person at the front desk was unhelpful. I don't know if his grasp of English was not good enough for him to understand what I was requesting (certainly my several words of Mandarin were insufficient), or if he simply wanted to protect the privacy of another guest. In any event, I didn't get any information on whether Tom was in the hotel or not. In fact, I had a feeling he wasn't. After a few bites of breakfast, the bus pulled up to take us to the exchange. I left decidedly worried. This was our first dealer exchange in Asia, and I was thrown a curve ball right off the bat.

The exchange was in English, almost all the managers spoke some, and it began with the local managers welcoming the dealers. At breaks and between speakers, the Chinese dealers talked among themselves in animated Mandarin, and I couldn't decide by looking at the body language if they were excited about what we were communicating or rejecting it out of hand.

I was on the agenda from 10:30 until noon discussing the new Implementation Guidebook we had created and presenting information on our hiring model, orientation, training and managing. Again, animated discussion occurred, and I had many thoughtful questions from the group. Tom didn't show up. At 11:45, about a 10-minute discussion in Mandarin took place, and as I stood in the front of the room, I glanced again at the agenda. The only item on the agenda after lunch was Tom. He started at 1 p.m. and he was slated to go until 5 p.m., with only a 15-minute coffee break in the middle.

I thought about all the weather and mechanical delays I'd suffered through in my international travels, perhaps the reception ran late and he missed the plane in St. Louis? Maybe his connection in Tokyo was canceled and he was languishing at Narita airport trying to figure out how to get to Shanghai? Why did I put my faith in three flight segments across half the globe? Maybe he was too fatigued from the wedding and the flight and was still sleeping in his hotel room?

If I was up to the plate all afternoon, surely, I'd strike out and embarrass the home team. At 11:55 a.m., just before we broke for lunch. Tom walked in. At lunch, he explained his flight had arrived late, and since he wasn't on the agenda until the afternoon, he chose to get a little more sleep.

He had about 15 PowerPoint slides, and began by saying "Ask a lot of questions, we have a lot of time." Before he left the third slide, two hours had passed. Every time he moved into another topic, hands would shoot up across the room and side conversations in Mandarin popped up. The local managers would receive gestures to join these conversations and for minutes at a time, Tom would be addressing one side of the room in English, while the other side slid into a conversation in Mandarin. When 5 p.m. arrived, he had two slides left. Conversation went far into extra innings.

The Chinese dealers were worried about the cultural fit. They explained that business in China was conducted face-to-face, not over the phone. Customers were reluctant to talk freely on the phone, both because of historical concerns about confidentiality, and the desire to meet the salesperson in person. As the initiative rolled out in China, they found that female inside sales representatives did well talking to the mostly male owner operators who had purchased equipment and now needed product support — parts and service. Tom made them feel comfortable by telling stories of how he overcame similar concerns within the southern culture of his dealership.

Mark Wankel had a colleague who also reported to Bob Morrisson named Erech Virden. Erech and I had worked together prior to this dealer exchange, and Erech was the kind of guy who could sit down in a crowded plane and know everyone by the time it landed. Erech had traveled with me to this dealer exchange because Mark was off on another assignment, and we decided to take the little free time we had and tour Shanghai.

As we walked in the People's Square, we were approached by three well-dressed Chinese who spoke excellent English and who wanted to take a picture of Erech — being that his reddish hair didn't look very Chinese. We struck up a conversation afterwards, and they invited us to tea.

Now I'm a cautious traveler, so I hung back a little, but Erech immediately said "Sure!" so off we went. Quickly the crowds thinned as we went into the back alleys of Shanghai. I was convinced I wouldn't see my family again and that I'd be found stuffed in some trash can on a side street. Finally, after about a 15-minute walk, we went up an exterior staircase into a doorway with Chinese written on it and into a small room.

We sat down at a table where a waitress soon appeared. Our host explained that as guests we could choose the number of teas for the ceremony. Since Erech and I were clueless, he selected seven teas. Each tea had a unique ceremony, and seven teas, we were soon to find out, is a lot of tea, so over the next two hours we had an elaborate ceremony for each tea with conversation between.

Our hosts were party members, obviously wealthy, with well-connected parents. They had a love for country as we did for ours, but no animosity or rivalry, just a genuine curiosity about life in the United States, and what we thought about China. I have no idea what this afternoon ended up costing, but they guided us back to the People's Square and we parted ways. Erech was energized — I thought we were lucky it worked out so well — and perhaps both of us were right.

We also did a dealer exchange in Geneva the same year. My wife and daughter went along so we could vacation for a few days when the exchange ended. Craig Putnal ("Caliper Boy") flew in one day and out the next to talk about personality profiling, and we brought Tom along for a dealer perspective, and his lovely wife, Judy. The Geneva office wanted a non-U.S. dealer to present as well, because they thought it would be more persuasive if the telephone sales concept was proven to work outside of the United States. So, I arranged for Sven who was the sales manager in Chile to join us. I had been to Sven's facility in Chile for sales training earlier. (Sven was named for a relative who emigrated from Sweden, but he was a native Chilean.)

Sixteen different dealers attended from all around Europe and as far away as South Africa and Egypt. Interest was growing exponentially. We had a lot of Caterpillar representatives join us as well, and I prepared a post-conference booklet that we distributed to both those who attended and dealers who couldn't make the trip.

During these dealer exchanges, both domestically and internationally, the issue of sales manager training became a critical topic of discussion. So in the summer of 2008, I began customizing our Leading High-Impact Telephone Sales Course for Caterpillar. The pilot was planned for the United Kingdom near Cannock in November, but in the meantime the economy began crashing in the United States and Europe. Mindful that telephone sales would build revenue during a time when revenue was desperately needed, the pilot went forward.

It was perhaps a bad omen for the upcoming economic gloom when I brought my computer audio speakers along from the United States and absent mindedly plugged them into the outlet in Cannock, only to hear a loud escalating squeal as the higher voltage trashed my speakers, setting off a mad dash to locate a pair that worked on English power voltage. The pilot went well, but during our trip to the U.K., Erech and I heard that all additional travel across the company would be canceled until further notice, and Barrack Obama had been elected President of the United States. The Great Recession had begun.

Chapter 16
DEMONSTRATE: The Collateral Presentation

When I began in field sales, we learned all the tricks of the collateral presentation. Gliding effortlessly between brochures, technical manuals, and PowerPoint slides, we wowed the buying committee. We trashed even the most obstinate price objections, ran roughshod over competitors, as if they didn't have a product worth mentioning or even comparing, and we closed the sales bacon. We brought the meaty commission home for our grateful families and fried it up in a pan. At least that's how I remember it. Reality, of course, was different.

The field salesperson has an easier time using collateral in a presentation because they are physically present and can control the environment, including what everyone is looking at and when materials are handed out. Perhaps most importantly, they can see the body language, and can interpret objections coming long before they're articulated.

The telephone salesperson must find a way to customize the collateral before sending it out. If they're mailing it out, a sticky note or marker will do. If they're emailing it out, markings on the PDF will work fine or bullet points in the email can be used. Customization should include the needs the customer has articulated, and should answer any risks. For example, if a salesperson is selling an engine rebuild to a trucking client, the needs may be, "You said you need to get back on the road quickly," and "You said controlling costs was important to you," plus "You said you wanted a great warranty." Risks might include, "Getting the appropriate credit for their old engine core" and achieving "long-term reliability."

The telephone salesperson should look over the literature and find references to as many of these risks and needs as possible before sending it to the prospect. Remember, risks are "uncertainty x impact on the business." Seeing something on paper or electronically reduces uncertainty, so the collateral presentation is a great way of dealing with risks. For needs, seeing something in writing makes the salesperson's words seem tangible and real.

Earlier I mentioned I completed my pilot's license to fly small planes. I bought a very used Piper Cherokee Warrior PA28-151 to cruise around the Midwest on sales calls during nice weather. I had a huge territory at the time and was booking over 50,000 miles a year by car. One night, I took the owner's manual of the plane home with me. I was reading about the operations of this plane, and it had a paragraph discussing what the author called a "flat spin." This is where the plane stalls and begins to orbit around the stalled wing. The paragraph ended by saying, "There is no known recovery." In other words, a crash is imminent.

A stall of the sales process is equally catastrophic, although financially rather than physically.

Most salespeople with consultant-sold product lose more sales to the stall — when the sales process just loses momentum and stops — than to "no." It is uniquely the salesperson's responsibility to manage the sales process in such a way that they get a "yes" or a "no." "No" may be caused by a pricing problem, a product problem or a positioning problem — issues jointly shared by the whole organization. But a stall is owned by the salesperson.

When sending out collateral, the best way to avoid a stall is to send it when the customer is on the phone and you have them engaged. But if the customer asks to review the information by themselves in between phone calls, the telephone sales representative must avoid the "collateral stall," when calling to see what the customer thought about what they sent:

Salesperson: "Have you had a chance to look over what I sent you?"

Customer: "Oh, I've been too busy. I haven't had a chance to look at it yet."

Salesperson: "Okay. Do you think you'll have time next week?"

Customer: "I'll try."

Salesperson: "I'll call you then."

What are the odds that Mr. or Ms. Customer will look over the collateral in the next week? Not good. If the salesperson calls again and they haven't had a chance to look at it, they'll feel guilty and avoid future calls. The salesperson is in the death spiral of the dreaded "collateral stall," with no known recovery. A better way is to call and say, "You asked me to send you some literature. What did you think?" Remember, it's good sales practice to sketch out the timeline once you generate interest, making sure the sales process is about the customer, not about the salesperson. This allows you to say, "You asked me to send you some literature," rather than "I sent you some literature."

"You" is much more powerful than "I."

Most customers will hem and haw, muttering something about not having had a chance to look at it. In which case, the salesperson should say, "I understand you've been busy. Why don't you pull it out right now? To save you time, I'll walk you through it." Most of the time, this works because almost everyone I've ever talked to in business-to-business selling is busy, and appealing to their lack of time is usually fruitful. Avoid the stall.

Once the telephone salesperson has the literature open and the customer's looking at it, he or she needs to present the benefits uncovered during the features, advantages, and benefits discussion, and point out the risks uncovered during the sales cycle probing — directing the customer to the place in the literature they have highlighted. In our example, the presentation might begin, "You said you need to get back on the road quickly. Look on page 3. I've highlighted our quick turnaround time."

You can continue by saying, "You said controlling costs were important to you. On page 5, I've highlighted a cost comparison with a rebuilt engine and a new and used engine, based on your truck model." Discussions on "a great warranty," "getting the appropriate credit for their old engine core," and "long-term reliability" would follow. This discussion will generate interest again, since the presentation is about the customer's specific needs. It will also likely lead to further discussions about other information contained in the collateral.

Another way a telephone salesperson can control the collateral presentation is to use a WebEx, Go-to-Meeting or other online presentation tool. The presentation method is the same, using prequalified benefit statements and dealing with articulated risk, however the stall risk is high, usually with the customer not showing up for the online presentation or cancelling at the last minute. The remedy is to generate sufficient interest. This is accomplished when the need is uncovered, and can be reinforced in writing between the first meeting and the online presentation.

The salesperson can send out a quick reminder email with the date and time, use the magic words, "You asked me to set up an online meeting. We agreed upon 2:00 this Tuesday." The email should also contain a few benefits to remind the customer of why they agreed to this meeting in the first place, and what additional information they will learn during this experience. The manager should carefully measure the success ratio of these meetings between representatives to cross-fertilize best practices and to keep stalls to a minimum. Sales is about both participating in the sales process (getting to a "yes" or a "no") and winning the deal (getting a "yes"). The selling organization closes exactly zero percent of the sales when they don't participate.

Many managers will find they can increase sales just as much by increasing participation as they can by winning a higher percentage of deals with a "yes" rather than a "no." How many sales cycles are going on today where the selling organization is not even at the table, because somewhere along the way the sales process stalled out? Either we didn't talk to the prospect at all, or we just quoted it and forgot it, or we sent them some literature and entered a death spiral, because they hadn't opened it when we called.

No known recovery.

Chapter 17
What Do You Think, Coach?

At Caterpillar, we adopted a three-pronged approach to training sales managers. First, we did annual dealer exchanges globally, which featured dealers talking to dealers. Mark would kick off each exchange by collecting the objectives of the group — why are you here? What would you like to learn? I would man the flip chart, documenting each bullet point, and Mark would mentally and physically check them off as each item was addressed.

The second prong was the implementation guidebooks. We made four revisions in these documents over the years. The last version was broken into specialty groups such as Power Systems, Machine Sales, Marine, Oil and Gas, and Product Support Machines, as more and more telephone sales representatives were added in each category. The implementation guidebooks had all the forms, documents, and instructions a manager would need to set up an effective inside sales operation. Of course, all the documents could be customized by each dealer.

The third prong was sales training, which we piloted in Cannock, England, just as the Great Recession kicked off. Sales is ultimately the concern of the manager, and he/she has multiple considerations to factor into their sales management style. By nature, the sales manager focuses on the performance of the overall department, while the salesperson is focused on closing the next deal. The sales manager who is only focused on helping their salespeople close the next deal is missing the huge impact they can have by designing a sales system which optimizes the chances for success.

Many sales managers were once the best salesperson in the department. And then, because they were the best, they were promoted to be manager. This would be like taking your best hitter in baseball and making him your third base coach. The sales manager who, as a super salesperson, will often think their best chance of hitting the sales target is to help representatives close their sales. In turn, they see themselves as the team closer. After all, this is where they've shined in the past. However, in a telephone-selling organization, where process, design, word choice, and the selection of salespeople is so critical, the sales manager can influence sales to a far greater degree by maximizing the sales system.

Early in my career, I had the opportunity to work in the one-day seminar industry. We mailed millions of four- and eight-page brochures a month, typically 15,000 to 20,000 per location. A response rate of about .6% was considered good, which resulted in 90 to 120 registrants. We sold on-site seminars over the phone, primarily from leads generated by the brochures, and sold product in the back of the room with our seminar presenter acting as a traveling field salesperson.

This experience, and my later experience at American Media managing the marketing and selling of training materials, reinforced for me the critical importance of integrating marketing with telephone sales.

Many sales managers are totally unprepared for managing a telephone selling function in business-to-business. If these managers have field sales experience, they are unaccustomed to the faster call rates in a telephone selling operation. They are also tuned to working with plentiful visual clues and with each representative being independent.

If their previous experience was in telemarketing, they may devalue the importance of relationship building and of open-dialogue conversations. If they were marketers, they may get the mechanics right, but not understand the emotional nutrition needs even a small staff of telephone sales representatives require, nor understand the dialogue dynamics of managing a sales cycle or presenting a complex product or service. Managing an open-dialogue telephone sales center is a specific and rather unique set of skills, combining sales and marketing.

Think of these management challenges. Telephone salespeople must invest a great deal of "emotional labor." Emotional labor is defined as expressing the desired emotion during a customer interaction. Think of the telephone sales job. The typical connection rate in business-to-business is about 20% — about one out of five times the telephone salesperson can get a decision maker on the phone. This means 80% of the time, the representative must emotionally gear themselves up — only to be disappointed. On the other 20% of the calls, where the representative gets someone on the line, they need to invest substantial emotional energy just to generate enough interest to continue the call, much less deal with objections, present the product or service, or ask for the sale. All the time they're doing this, they're sitting in a cubicle or some other stationary setting, with a lack of new visual clues.

Consider burnout. Often clients worry about it or have problems with telephone sales representative burnout. Won't a telephone salesperson get burned out quickly and need to move on? Burnout has less to do with overwork than powerlessness — working hard and being surrounded by circumstances that don't make sense. If the telephone salesperson doesn't have the right positioning or the right call outlines, doesn't get lead support, and has customers that don't get what they are promised, they will burn out.

Now, some of this is part of the job, of course. No manager can write call outlines that cover the depth and breadth of the typical database. Not every customer will be 100% satisfied all the time. But burnout is an accumulation of a thousand cuts over time. I know telephone sales representatives who have over 20 years on the job. What's not to like? They're out of the cold, and they're home on time every night. They're not caught like the poor field sales guy miles away from home at the end of the day. Why should they burn out? Burnout is usually a problem of getting the management right.

What about activity levels? How many calls should each representative make per day? When I arrived at American Media, the call quota was 20 calls per day. I gradually raised the call quota to 60 calls per day. As I did, revenue went up proportionally. At some level, telephone sales is a numbers game. I'd rather have a salesperson that closed 20% of their deals, but did the dials so they participated in $2,000,000 a year ($400,000 in new revenue), than have a representative that closed 40%, but only participated in $500,000 ($200,000 in new revenue), because they only called a few select customers. What about talk time? A world-class level is 150 minutes, but what works in each individual business should be set by the manager. What other activities are appropriate? For example, the number of proposals, achieving a planned annual rate of call (PAR), or percentage of inbound calls as a proxy for the strength of the relationship, or perhaps others? All of these are set by the manager.

Selection is also critical. Not everyone can do this job. Some applicants will come into the telephone selling organization, shadow an existing representative, and say, "This is not for me." Others will interview as champs, but perform as chumps. The manager must have a selection process that weeds out applicants who can't do the job, and raises up those who can.

Onboarding, orientation, and training are required. Once a new telephone salesperson is hired, how do managers set their role perceptions, provide product and/or service training and sales training? The telephone was invented in 1876, but human beings have been talking face-to-face for millennia. Our engrained intuition is wrong for telephone sales. Engage in small talk first? Not on the phone.

Generate interest first. Small talk comes when the relationship is established. Talk extensively about the product? Not on the phone. You need to work in those small bites of product information into your dialogue. Talking too long at one time on the phone will cause your customer to fall asleep. The manager must have a good training process.

The manager must answer questions. First, the manager should create effective policies that answer most reoccurring questions. Second, the manager is the representative from the sales department to the rest of the organization, and the manager must be responsible for taking care of operational problems. The manager is also a coach, raising the performance of lower performers up to the standards of the top performers.

In a nutshell, the sales manager stands between the telephone salesperson and the organization, and needs to be able to: A) Design a business model that will generate the results required within an acceptable cost-of-sales budget; B) Plan sales activities (e.g., positioning, call outlines, activity goals); C) Select the right employees; D) Orient and train representatives, both reoccurring training for experienced representatives and onboarding for new reps; E) Create effective policies, which are standing answers to reoccurring questions and constraints on the activities of the telephone salespeople (e.g., pricing, credit terms and product adjustments); F) Coach telephone salespeople to close the gap between high and low performers; G) Provide emotional nutrition to balance the emotional labor invested by the salesperson, and H) Solve operational problems between the telephone salesperson's customers and the organization.

Business Model

Begin with marketing. In conjunction with his or her marketing department, the telephone sales manager should survey the landscape of customers and prospects and set realistic coverage goals. Which accounts should be assigned to a representative? Which accounts should be handled by marketing only? And which accounts should be assigned to field sales, if relevant?

The critical metric is the increase in revenue that can logically be estimated, given the additional sales pressure. Accounts below this threshold should be assigned to marketing to nurture. For example, if the group of accounts assigned to a telephone sales representative is currently generating $2 million in revenue, and the representative can increase sales by 20% by building relationships and applying sales pressure, $400,000 of additional revenue will be gained. If the selling organization's cost-of-goods-sold is 25%, and the total cost of the telephone sales representative, plus overhead and management costs, is $100,000; that means the organization will realize $200,000 of gross profit. The effort is worthwhile.

What if the telephone sales representative is plowing a green field and starting a territory with no existing revenue? Using the business case above, is it realistic they can sell $400,000 of products or services with only personal selling, or will marketing need to help generate leads? Too often, telephone sales initiatives fail because lead generation is not factored in, thus the telephone representative starves trying to kick up enough action on their own.

The manager needs to be realistic. What can be accomplished by personal selling, and what lead generation needs to take place? Using our example again, 25% of revenue is cost-of-goods, 25% ($100,000/$400,000) is cost-of-sales. Can the organization allocate $60,000 to lead generation, or 15% of revenue? The resulting business model would be: 25% cost of goods + 25% cost of sales + 15% cost of marketing = 65% for a gross profit of 100% - 65% = 35%.

What is an acceptable business model for your organization? The hardest part of telephone selling is to generate initial interest, and cold calling may be the most expensive way of doing it. If cold calling is the only way to generate initial interest because the opportunity is high and the database is small, so be it. But otherwise, your business model should contain a realistic dose of marketing.

Consideration should also be given to participation. How many sales cycles are going on out there that the selling organization is not participating in? The manager must then set the positioning as we discussed earlier, and develop the call outlines. Like any good marketer, the manager should test positioning to determine what works best, and do A/B splits to determine quantitatively what works best.

The manager should set the planned annual rate of call (PAR). Typically the rate should be at least four to maintain a relationship, but more, if necessary, for product or service support or business needs. The manager should set activity levels such as the number of calls per day each representative will attempt, and the talk time they should achieve. At some level, telephone selling is a numbers game, and if the organization doesn't make the dials, it won't win.

Selection

The salesperson immediately impressed me. Whether it was the firm handshake, the spot-on appropriate dress, the eye contact, or the iron-clad resume, I don't know. But his name immediately went to the top of the pile. His face-to-face interview went fabulously. I found myself spending more time on selling him on why he should work here than on finding out if he was qualified. Others interviewed, but they just didn't stack up. I kept thinking, this is the guy.

But he wasn't. It became apparent once he started that he was restless and wouldn't make the dials. There was always some reason he needed to be out of his cubicle and in someone else's business. When I listened to conversations with customers, they were okay. But there weren't enough of them to really make a difference. He was poor at prospecting and in executing the sales process that I knew would work. "I just have my own way of doing it. It works. It always has," he told me. It didn't work this time, and we parted ways.

What I learned is selection is critical. Mark Wankel and I talked about this a great deal, and he would stand up at dealer exchanges and say, "If you don't want to hire the right person, stop. Don't go any further. You'll be disappointed and blame the program." In essence, I've found the universe of people who can be successful at telephone sales is narrower than those that can be successful in customer service or field sales, but someone who is successful at telephone sales can probably excel in either customer service or field sales.

The customer service representative doesn't need to generate initial excitement. The customer is already interested or they wouldn't have picked up the phone and called. The field salesperson generates initial excitement just by showing up. The field salesperson is physically and visually present. Telephone salespeople have none of this going for them. They need to generate excitement in the first seconds of the call, or it is game over. Unless you have dialed the phone 60 times a day or more and had this responsibility, it's hard to know how emotionally draining this is.

Some people have the intestinal fortitude to do this and others don't. It's not a bad thing if you don't, but telephone sales is simply not the right job for you. Others emotionally can do the call opening, but struggle with being in an environment all day with a lack of visual clues. The cubicle looks the same on Monday as it does on Friday. The only thing that changes is the words on the computer screen.

If you're lucky enough to have a window, the changing seasons beyond also provide a change of pace. Others struggle with a repetitive job, and picking up the phone over 60 times a day and talking to only 20% of those you call. If you can't stand voicemail, if you can't stand someone telling you Mr. or Ms. Jones is in a meeting, this isn't the job for you.

Some applicants have too much customer empathy. Not only do they always side with the customer against the selling organization, they are vocal about it, creating discord and bringing down other departments on the sales manager's head. Other applicants are so customer-service oriented, they can't ask for the sale. They genuinely build a good relationship, but just send out quotes, hoping beyond reasonable hope that the customer will like them enough to buy without being asked. Others talk way too much; they upend the 60%-customer-talk, 40%-salesperson-talk rule, and drown out even customers who are most disposed to buy with verbiage.

Bill Buss and I agree on the metrics. When we hire, it's about one out of 70 applicants. I used to hire a much higher percentage. But experience — the most expensive teacher there is — has broken me of that practice. As a manager, I learned that each hour invested in good salesperson selection was worth five hours of management and coaching. The best advice I ever got on marriage was, "Don't think you can change him or her after you exchange vows. Personality is permanent." The same is true in telephone sales. You can teach technique to someone who has demonstrated a willingness to learn in their life, and you can coach someone who has demonstrated they are adaptable.

You can't change the telephone salesperson whose personality won't generate excitement, who can't stomach only talking to 20% of the people they dial, who needs different visual stimulus daily, who can't do a repetitive job, who believes the customer is always right — regardless of the circumstances or cost, and who can't ask for the sale, or finally, talks too much. It's almost impossible to change these engrained personality traits. It doesn't make people who do these things bad. Telephone sales is just not the job for them. We have a nine-step selection model:

1. Advertising and Recruiting
2. Resume Screening
3. Telephone Screening
4. Face-to-Face Interview
5. Assessment
6. Secondary Face-to-Face Interview
7. Job Shadowing
8. Reference Checking
9. Offer

The goal is to screen out those who can't do the job, and pick the best one who can.

Advertising and Recruiting

Who do you want on the telephone selling team?

Aptitudes are the innate personality characteristics of an individual. Aptitudes are expressed in behaviors in given situations. Think of the wide variety of people you know. Each person is unique, with different personality characteristics that define how they interact with other people and how well they will perform in a job. Aptitudes are difficult to change, and therefore, people with the right aptitudes for the telephone selling job need to be selected. Competencies on the other hand are defined by Training Magazine as a cluster of related knowledge, attitudes, and skills that affect a major portion of a job. Competencies can be improved through orientation into the selling organization, training, coaching, mentoring, and job experiences.

The most successful hiring posture is to select individuals with the best aptitudes for the telephone sales job, and then develop competencies within these individuals to suit. Sometimes managers need to make compromises, selecting individuals who have industry and product knowledge because they have worked other positions within the selling organization such as customer service. The danger for the hiring manager is that sub-optimal aptitudes are extremely difficult to change, and often place a low bar on ultimate performance. Competencies can be changed, and require an investment of the organization's money and probably the sales manager's time. However, this investment pales next to the superior sales the best aptitude telephone salespeople will deliver after his or her competencies are raised. The best practice is to hire for aptitude and train for competencies.

A good place to start is gathering referrals from your employee base. Does someone know someone who has the aptitude for the job? Customers may also be open to providing referrals. A second source of new telephone sales representatives is competitors, which is fairly risky, but often used by selling organizations. A key consideration is this — if the person is willing to jump from a competitor to your organization, will he or she also be willing to jump again if another offer surfaces? This is a question best resolved on a case-by-case basis by reviewing the person's past work history and the reason for leaving the competitor's workforce.

Resume Screening

The next step is to create a spreadsheet of all the applicants and begin rating them quantitatively. As you go through the next steps, you will start to see some applicants rising to the top, literally, if you sort your spreadsheet. The goal is to take as much qualitative judgement out of the process that you can, and make the process more than a gut feeling (this is an inside joke for me, our bestselling video at American Media was "More Than A Gut Feeling").

I typically create a rating form evaluating customer and technical skills. Think of the resume you receive as an advertisement for the applicant. Don't be overly impressed by the writing style or the physical appearance of the resume. Rather, try to maintain your focus on the content. Professional writers can take almost any background and make it look magnificent. But they can't change the factual underpinnings.

Look for positive signs — experience that indicates specific accomplishments and obstacles overcome on the job, accomplishments that come with clear revenue results, career progressions that indicate progress rather than just hopping around, and evidence of technical expertise such as licenses, certificates or work history. Also, look for undesirable signs — descriptions of jobs that are hazy, ill-defined and include qualifying phrases which may indicate brief exposure but not expertise. Look for disorganized information, unexplained gaps in employment history, information that is not work related or does not relate to the telephone sales position.

I usually create a Resume Screening Tool (See Sample Document 17-02 on BPGrp.com) to assist in this process. This document allows you to score each resume quantitatively. Once you've done this, divide the spreadsheet with the names into three groups: 1) Candidates — the most attractive and viable folks who applied — perhaps 30% to 40% of the original group; 2) The "maybes" — backup candidates who possess some of the important requirements and could be potentially developed for the job; and 3) The "knockouts" — those candidates who, because of background, salary requirements or experience, are not a fit for your organization.

Telephone Screening

The next step is phone screening. If the person can't sell themselves to the manager, how will they sell the selling organization's products or services? Any individual who fits into the definite candidates above should go through this step. The purpose of the 10- to 15-minute call is to screen out applicants who are not a fit. I typically develop a telephone screening form for this. (See Sample Document 17-03 at BPGrp.com.) Good practice is to ask the candidate to sell you on why they should be invited in for a face-to-face interview.

The candidate should ask questions around the selling organization's needs, and then position their background as a fit. Now they'll be nervous, and on the spot. So don't expect polish or perfection. But expect a good attempt. The goal of telephone screening is to select the top 30% to advance to the face-to-face interview. Again, collect the quantitative results from the telephone screening form and put the numbers in your spreadsheet, and select the successful candidates from there.

Face-to-Face Interview

By this time, the manager has talked to everyone during the phone interview, and reviewed their resume. The interview should take place in a neutral location, if possible. I recommend a behavioral-based interview, because past behavior is the best predictor of future behavior. These questions typically start like, "Tell me about a time when..."

Typically, the manager will ask 15 to 20 questions during an hour-long interview. Each candidate should receive the same core group of questions. The face-to-face interview form allows the manager to come up with a number again which should be added to the spreadsheet. (See Sample Document 17-04 at BPGrp.com.) If the responses from a candidate are unclear, ask additional questions from the interview form until you can rate the candidate.

Assessment

After the face-to-face interviews, you will probably have two to three serious candidates. These applicants should be given a valid personality assessment to learn about their aptitudes and innate talents. At Caterpillar, we used the Caliper assessment, helpfully introduced by "Caliper Guy" Craig Putnal. There are others available in the marketplace. We found Caliper to be superior for telephone sales in our assessment. It was so effective that for years Caterpillar supplemented the costs for dealers who were beginning a telephone selling operation. One of the early tasks I did with Caterpillar was to determine an inside telephone selling profile. (See Sample Document 17-05 at BPGrp.com.)

Secondary Face-to-Face Interview

Once you have the assessment back, and have all the quantitative evaluations on your spreadsheet, usually the superior candidate is obvious. The secondary interview allows you to integrate all the data gathered in the previous steps and to ask questions around any weaknesses found. The sales manager may want to bring other managers into this interview.

Job Shadowing

If possible, it is recommended that the successful candidate shadow existing telephone salespeople. (This is not possible on the first hire of course.) Some candidates may decline to be hired after seeing what the job entails. Shadowing allows you to also quiz the representative being shadowed. Did the applicant ask intelligent questions about the position? Do they seem like a good cultural fit? How was their communication style?

Reference Checking

The next step is to check references. In today's litigious society, many previous employers will only confirm dates of employment. If you can, talk to the supervisor of the candidate. Try to verify the resume, look for inflated job histories or salaries. Typically, a positive statement followed by a question is helpful in this process. Positive statement: "Mr. Applicant appears to be a real follower of the rules who wants to be 100% correct and at the same time, achieve superior results." Question: "How did he manage tough deadlines?"

Job Offer

Congratulations! The manager has selected a telephone salesperson, chosen because they have the best aptitude for the job! The offer should include a compensation plan, the selling organization's benefit package, and a Personal Business Plan. (Sample Document 17-06 at BPGrp.com.) The Personal Business Plan includes the activities required (e.g., calls per day, talk time) and the results expected (e.g., revenue, proposals).

Orientation

The largest motivating factor for a telephone salesperson is how clear their sales tasks are and the direct relationship between the effort they expend and their sales result. Clarity begins with orientation, which begins the minute the new telephone sales representative joins the selling organization, and continues with training. For the purposes of this book, I will refer to "orientation" as the selling organization-facing items such as the Personal Business Plan, and the policies and procedures of the selling organization. "Training" will refer to customer-facing skills such as the five steps of the sales system presented in this book, DISCOVER – DESIGN – DEMONSTRATE – CLOSE – CHECK, as well as industry orientation and customer knowledge.

The Personal Business Plan (Sample Document 17-06 at BPGrp.com) describes the activities required of the telephone salesperson every day, as well as the sales results expected over time, which is typically the revenue they generate. A telephone salesperson has under their control the activities they do each day, while sales results are somewhat unpredictable day-to-day, because they also depend on the customer. The sales manager can monitor daily activities and can listen to phone calls. If the calls follow the sales model, and the activities are met, the sales manager can be reasonably assured the results targets will be hit if they were calculated per the business model.

Because there is often a significant lag time between an activity and the sales result, and the beginning of any sales cycle and the end, the failure to achieve the daily activity goals is a huge red flag that poor results may be on the way. Because the largest motivating factor for a telephone salesperson is how clear their sales tasks are, and the direct relationship between the effort they expend and their sales result, the manager should carefully explain where the activity requirements come from, and how they relate to results.

The new telephone salesperson should also be introduced to members of the selling organization he or she will need to communicate with to do his or her job. This may include customer service, fulfillment, service delivery, and marketing. In my experience, about 15% of the typical 25-working day onboarding process is invested directly in this type of orientation. Your onboarding process may be longer or shorter depending on your product and/or service complexity. The remainder of the onboarding process will be human resource related, shadowing existing representatives, and training.

Training

Training consists of market, customer, and industry orientation (typically about 20% of the onboarding time), selling techniques (25%), and product and/or service knowledge (40%). Customer orientation should include a detailed study of the assigned territory. Bill Buss taught me a great technique. He had his telephone salespeople do a territory analysis. They'd go online and research major customers and what was going on in the geographic area of the territory, if applicable. He'd ask the new representative to come back and do a summary for him to show they understood. The sales manager should also assure that the new telephone sales representative clearly understands what his or her customers do, and how they use the products and services of the selling organization. Industry orientation includes the competitive landscape, including how the products and services of competitors stack up against the offerings of the selling organization.

Product and service knowledge is what the telephone sales representative will be selling. A good way to acquire product knowledge is to create a feature-and-questions matrix as presented in Chapter 4. New representatives should learn product in the same way they will be selling the product.

There is no need to get too technical, especially during orientation, if engineering details never come up during a sales conversation. Good practice includes doing a similar feature matrix for competitive product, but instead of questions, including a column for responses. In this way, the salesperson will be prepared for customer objections derived from competitive product.

Sales knowledge can be learned online, and it is the most cost-effective way to acquire the knowledge. We have broken down the sales process into defined competencies and online training modules:

• Systems Proficiency
• Qualifying
• Cross- and Up-Selling
• Customer Care
• Continuous Learning
• Opportunity Generation
• Outbound Telephone Selling
• Customer Business
• Product and Solution Understanding
• Value Proposition
• Time Management
• Handling Objections
• Sales Opportunity Management
• Relationship Development
• Consultative Selling
• Closing
• Communication
• Territory Planning
• Account Development

This is followed by two intensive days of skills training called High-Impact Telephone Sales. During skills training, the telephone sales representatives follow the DISCOVER – DESIGN – DEMONSTRATE – CLOSE – CHECK model with abundant exercises and role-plays to cement what they've learned. After this sales training, we typically immediately put the new representative on the phone and provide coaching to assure the skills were acquired and bad habits are not started. (See Document 17-07 at BPGrp.com.)

To be a private pilot, you need about 12 to 16 hours with an instructor before you solo, and at least 40 hours to take the flight test. We follow a similar pattern in sales training with two days — 16 hours — of skill instruction before going on the phone, and another three days before the new telephone representative solos on their own. Forty hours to takeoff!

Coaching

In high school, I had a teacher who made a huge impact on the trajectory of my life. Eugene Eckhoff was an English teacher, but in reality, he was a life coach. I took as many courses as I could from him, including creative writing. As I planned my career in engineering and business, creative writing was a stretch, but he constantly encouraged all of us to expand the boundaries of our imagination and writing. No effort was bad, unless it was obviously quickly and thoughtlessly done, but every piece of writing could be improved, and he coached and cajoled and stretched and poked and prodded. The end products were substantially better than the effort with which I started.

Think about a good coach you have worked with in your life. Who would that person be? The band director who helped you discover the difference between music and noise? Perhaps the physics teacher who revealed the secrets of the universe where only complex equations existed before? The mechanic who taught you that any problem can be solved? Your first boss?

What made this person special?

A great coach provides leadership and helps others improve. "Telephone sales coaching" is very important to the telephone sales representative and helps the selling organization build a department of superior sales folks. Coaching is one of those rare interventions that influences role perception, skill levels, and motivation levels. Coaching raises skill levels by pointing out what was observed and comparing it to best practices. And coaching boosts motivation because of the investment of one-on-one time.

All this said, conducting coaching is costly in terms of the sales manager's time. One-on-one time provides the sales manager with little time leverage across the department. Therefore, coaching should not be used as a substitute for a good management system to promote and reward activities. Coaching should focus on improving the behaviors that directly impact sales results.

Observation plays a key role in the coaching process. Observing a telephone sales representative typically means shadowing when he or she is making telephone calls or listening to taped conversations. Although if you use call taping, make sure you comply with your state's regulations regarding the practice. The benefit of shadowing is that the manager can watch the telephone representative perform all the activities required to work the territory.

Once the sales manager has observed a series of sales conversations, he or she should praise the telephone sales representative for three things and identify three areas for improvement. While the sales manager may identify five or six areas that need improvement during any given observation session, I recommend these be narrowed down to the three areas of biggest impact. Changing behavior is difficult, and the coach does not want to make it overwhelming.

When I began Business Performance Group in 2000, I started out as a sales coach and I thoroughly enjoyed it. As time passed, I recognized that many items of praise and improvement items keep coming up again and again, so I created a database of typical observations, along with praise statements that can be used if the telephone sales representative is executing the skill well and improvement statements to use if the representatives needs to develop the skill. (See Document 17-08 at BPGrp.com.)

After you've identified the praise and improvement items, a development plan should be created. (See Document 17-09 at BPGrp.com.) Since the development plan requires the sales manager coach and the telephone representative to act, it should be signed by both. The representative will need to master the improvement items outlined in the plan. The sales manager coach will need to follow up to see that improvement is made.

The sales manager may coach an experienced telephone sales representative only once a quarter. For a new representative, coaching may take place every other week. When it comes to coaching, don't ignore your top performers — the superstars. Experience has shown that the easiest telephone sales representatives to coach are the top performers and those that are new to the position. Top performers appreciate any edge that makes them better and puts money in their pockets. New telephone sales representatives are often eager for any advice they can get, and perhaps a little scared. It is the "mediocre middle" who struggle with coaching. Their egos may be fragile enough that any constructive comments are perceived as criticism.

For many years, I coached Rocky White's sales staff at National Seminars Group. Rocky, as I mentioned earlier, hosted the training session when Mark Wankel from Caterpillar wanted to preview the course. The high performers in Rocky's telephone sales center were the "Million Dollar Club" who generated over that amount per year in new revenue. Rocky allowed his sales representatives to sign up for coaching when I came down, and my dance card was always full of "Million Dollar Club" members. As I listened, and made suggestions on handling an objection, or perhaps a little better way to leave a voicemail, they would smile, jot it down, and thank me when I left. They didn't need an ego boost; they just wanted an edge to get that next sale.

There were some representatives who had been around for some time who never asked for coaching. They hovered right above the minimum sales requirement to stay on the team and constituted Rocky's "mediocre middle." If someone started slipping down below the minimum, Rocky would put them on my list. Some would take advice and would be there the next time I came back; others wouldn't and would be gone.

I noticed a pattern, those in the "Million Dollar Club" always did the activities required to do the job, and so did the new representatives. The newbies did the activities because they were scared. The "Million Dollar Club" did the activities because they knew they worked. Some of the "mediocre middle" did the activities. Some didn't. The representatives who didn't do the activities either started doing them or were gone. Almost every member of the "mediocre middle" that did the activities, and took coaching seriously, grew beyond bouncing at the cut line and they became productive members of the department.

These coaching experiences at National Seminars and elsewhere led me to create the following model:

"D" Representatives	"C" Representatives	"B" Representatives	"A" Representatives
NOT doing activities NOT achieving results	DOING activities NOT achieving results	NOT doing activities ACHIEVING results	DOING activities ACHIEVING results

The sales manager coaches the high performers for retention, to provide the "Atta boy," and "Atta girl," positive reinforcement and to give them an edge. The sales manager coaches the "B" representative for motivation. The manager might say, "What could you be doing representative 'B' if you actually did all the required activities, such as number of calls and phone time?" Did the "B" representative have a large sale, a bluebird that just flew in his or her sales window, and as soon as that sale passes in the rearview mirror they will fall to a "D?" These "B" representatives are in danger of future results problems.

The "C" representatives are doing the activities but not achieving the results. Here the sales manager can coach for sales skills and typically get a big boost in performance. The "D" representatives will never be successful unless they start first doing the activities. So this is primarily a discipline problem. Start doing the activities.

This matrix allows the sales manager to focus their time. Coach the "A" high performers quarterly to keep them contented and on the phone and to provide a new edge. Coach the "B" to get their activities up, or look at the goals. Are the goals too low for this territory? Invest time in the "C" representatives for skill improvement and put the "D" representatives on notice.

Coaching Model — The Coaching Conversation

Our coaching model is based on five phases:

• Contracting

• Observation and Action

• Commitment and Achieve

The first phase, Contracting, involves establishing a mutual understanding of expectations between the telephone salesperson and the sales manager. Previously, I discussed how the Personal Business Plan can establish the primary role perception for the salesperson. This document is the sales manager's basis for establishing a "contract" between themselves and the telephone sales representative — an understanding of the expectations of the job.

During orientation, the sales manager will want to review the Personal Business Plan with the new representative. Annually or semi-annually new plans should be prepared. Sales goals should be calculated first, and then activity goals derived from the results required.

The second phase is Observation, and is the quantitative and qualitative measurement of how the representative is performing against the expectations established in the Personal Business Plan. Quantitative measurements are evaluations of actual activities and results compared to the Plan. Qualitative measurements will require the sales manager coach to observe the salesperson performing his or her job.

I typically shadow a telephone sales representative for exactly an hour. At the end of the hour, I can take the number of dials and multiply by eight and tell the representative what their call rate is. I can also talk to them about the number of decision makers they talked to, how many gatekeepers, and how many voicemails. Usually reps are surprised at the number of dials they make when being shadowed, normally it's 12 to 15 dials. They're also usually surprised by the number of decision makers they talk to — usually 2 to 3 — the typical 20%.

Most of the time they'll turn to me and say, "I hardly got a hold of anybody." This gives me plenty of ammunition to tell the representative who is only making 50 dials a day to say, "You did 15 dials an hour with me. Over an eight-hour day. That's 120." Or, if they complain that they only got a hold of 10 people today, I can say, "You got a hold of three people with me during the hour we sat together. That's 24 a day." It's amazing how having someone sit and listen to your calls focuses the mind.

The third phase is Action. Action includes the steps required to bring what is observed up to expectation. The sales manager's primary benchmark for action will be the Personal Business Plan — the contract. If the sales manager observes something not at the level of the Personal Business Plan, the action phase defines the required effort needed to bring performance up to the expected level.

At the end of the shadowing, collect the things you saw that went well, as well as the areas of improvement, and create a Development Plan. The next step is to sit down with the representative and explain what you saw, and the improvement actions you'd like them to take. This might be a typical conversation:

Sales manager: "First of all, I really like the way you handled gatekeepers on your calls. You always tried to build a relationship, and you always tried to find out something about the business to warm up the next call. I also want to compliment you on exploring the business issues with customer "x." I thought you did a good job of finding out their current policy expires in six months. Finally, you have a great tone of voice on the phone. You sound interested in their business and in solving problems for the customer. Good job!"

Representative: "Thanks! I find gatekeepers do give a lot of information if you just ask and treat them with respect. Customer "x" sounds like a good prospect and I'll be working this lead."

Sales manager: "Great. What else did you notice?"

Representative: "I thought I blew quite a few calls. The call with customer "y" didn't go very well and I don't think I'm where I need to be with customer "z.""

Sales manager: "Oh, I didn't think it went that badly. I did find a few areas where I'd like us to work together to improve. I think this will help you close more business. First, you had the opportunity with customer "y" to determine their buying committee. Don't be afraid to find out who else may be influencing their purchasing decisions. Second, when you talked to customer "z," I felt you didn't really propose any next steps. Without defined next steps, the sales cycle may stall. Third, with customer "z," I noticed you didn't establish their timeline which is when they need the product. Overall an excellent job, though. You had some great calls. And these improvements will make a major impact on your results."

Representative: "Thanks."

My experience is that telephone sale representatives will be harder on themselves than you will be. After you finish shadowing, ask them how it went. They'll tell you. It will usually be a negative self-assessment. And then you can pick them up off the floor with a few constructive ways to get better, beginning first with praise. Bill Buss will ask after shadowing, "What did you do well?" Once he sees what the representative thought went well, he'll fill in with his statements of praise. Then he'll ask, "If you could do it all over again, what would you do differently?" The representative will then list what they think they did that was not as effective, and the manager coach can provide their feedback.

What makes a good action step? A good action step provides specific direction to the telephone sales representative on what they can do differently. For example, if the coach observes "probing for buying committee," the action step may be, "Ask about the buying committee to identify all the potential decision makers — formal or informal." If, on the other hand, the coach observes the representative had done a great job of identifying the buying committee, the praise statement could be, "<Name> probes for the buying committee and finds out all the individuals affected by the business issue." Here are three examples from the "Skills Database" (see Document 17-08 at BPGrp.com):

Description	Praise	Development Action
Probing for Buying Committee	<Name> probes for the buying committee and finds out all the individuals affected by the business issue.	Ask about the buying committee to identify all the potential decision makers — formal or informal.
Call Conclusion	<Name> establishes good "next steps" on each call. These steps advance the sales process.	On each call, make sure you establish the "next steps" of the sales process.
Probing for Timeline	<Name> probes for timeline effectively and uses the information to guide and manage the sales process.	Probe for timeline. Use the information to manage the sales cycle and plan the investment of your time.

Notice that I "personalize" the praise by using the representative's name. Action steps alone are not enough. For a representative to make a behavior change, they need to also know the "why." Why is the manager, my coach asking me to make this change? The "Development Action Plan" provides the "why," and "Outcomes" tells the representative the positive impact this change will have on their sales performance:

Description	Development Action Plan	Outcomes
Probing for Buying Committee	Many individuals may have an impact on your ability to sell a particular solution. By probing for the buying committee, you have a much better chance to address the needs, timelines, and risks of everyone who will have input into the choice of your solution. Your job is to sell to everyone who has a voice in the decision-making process.	When you identify the buying committee, you will identify all of the risks, needs, and timelines, leading to higher sales.
Call Conclusion	When you establish "next steps" at the end of each sales call, you can open your next call with, "You said ..." or "You asked me to ..." or similar language. This makes the call about the buyer, not about you. Your job as a salesperson is to manage the sales cycle. Establish next steps — do your homework — and use the references to "you said" as your next compelling reason to call.	By determining next steps, you will advance the sales cycle, which leads to the money call — where you ask for the sale.
Probing for Timeline	Timeline is important in business-to-business. When does the buyer see solving the business issue? Sometimes the need is immediate. At other times it is long term. By probing for timeline, you will be able to manage the sales process and your time effectively.	When you probe for timeline, you will manage both your time and the buyer's. This will lead to more efficiency and higher sales.

The fourth phase is Commitment. Commitment is the agreement to take the steps required to bring what is observed up to expectation. Think about it. Do you make New Year's Eve resolutions? How many of those do you accomplish? If you are like me, most New Year's Eve resolutions end up being reluctantly disregarded because it's so difficult to change our own behavior. If it's hard to change our own behavior, just think how much more difficult it is to change someone else's behavior.

In coaching, you're asking a telephone sales representative to change their behavior in an emotional heightened situation — when they are on the phone with a customer. They're already investing a significant amount of emotional labor, and changing behavior requires more effort. This is difficult work, and won't happen unless the representative totally commits to the task. Change is hard, and it's very easy to fall back into the same habits. Therefore, the coach should focus on no more than three improvement actions at a time.

At our "boot camps" for telephone sales representatives, I debrief with representatives after each call if warranted. Even on the next call, right after our discussion, the representative will often repeat the same mistake. And, of course, I'm listening and sitting right beside them. It's extremely difficult to change behavior in an emotionally charged atmosphere like a customer call. Earlier, I noted how important selecting for the right aptitudes is so important, because aptitudes are so hard to change. Aptitudes are especially hard to change during emotional, laborious customer calls.

For example, it's far easier to get telephone sales representatives with the appropriate aptitude of empathy to ask more open-ended questions (a competency). They are predisposed to listen anyway, not talk over customers, and want to learn about the individual on the other end of the line. When the coach provides a better technique for doing so, they're motivated to learn and apply the new skill. Even so, changing behavior is still hard.

I use a "Business Development Plan" to gain commitment. This plan includes "praise statements" of noteworthy accomplishments the coach observed, "development actions" for improvements, "action plans" which contain the methodology to address the needed improvements, "outcomes" which are the positive results the representative will see when they make the change, "achieving the goals" which are resources the rep can use to accomplish the action plan and "follow up activities," which is the time when the coach and rep will discuss the changes made.

I think having a follow up meeting is critical. The follow-up meeting commits the coach to do something — to hold this meeting. And it tells the representative that the coaching session is just not a "one and done," but a process with change expected by a certain date. At the bottom of the "Business Development Plan" is the place for the manager coach and representative to sign or initial, indicating their mutual commitment. Documentation, mutual tasks, and a clear pathway of what actions to take are critical. (See Document 17-09 at BPGrp.com.)

The final phase is Achieve. Achieve involves the tools and resources a salesperson needs to take the necessary steps to bring their observed behavior up to expectations. In the "Skills Database," I've linked each action plan back to a specific module of our e-learning programs. The goal is to provide the representative with a place to learn, or re-learn — how to do the actions the coach is requesting.

Often, I've had managers say, "I've never sold on the phone before. How can I coach?" If you haven't, just listen carefully to the sales conversation. You can use the "Skills Database" to take what you've heard and make it concrete. Unlike the telephone sales representative, you can listen intently to both sides of the conversation. The rep must keep the conversation going, so their brain is focused both on the customer and what they will say or ask next. The coach doesn't have that constraint. Even an inexperienced observer can uncover improvements, just by listening carefully to the conversation.

Managing

Managing a business-to-business telephone sales department is a difficult task. First, there are the human needs — selection, orientation, coaching, providing emotional nutrition, and being the interface with the rest of the organization. Second, there are the more structural issues — establishing the business model, defining territories, activities, and results for each salesperson, and developing and communicating policies.

The sales manager is responsible for solving operational problems between the telephone salesperson's customers and the organization, and for representing the telephone sales department to the rest of the organization. No delivery model works well 100% of the time. Customers will occasionally be disappointed, and the first person they usually call is the salesperson who has established a relationship. In fact, the more effective the telephone sales representatives have been in establishing a relationship, the more likely they are to be the first contact the customer makes when something doesn't go as planned.

In some instances, the rep can directly take care of the problem. An item damaged in transit can be replaced, a missed appointment can be rescheduled, or an item can be returned. Systemic problems however, are the responsibility of the sales manager to address. In most organizations, the telephone salesperson does not have sufficient status to address systemic problems, and may be seen as a pest or a nuisance if they persist. The sales manager, due to their status as a manager, does have organizational heft to do this heavy lifting.

The sales manager will typically coordinate with marketing on lead-generating programs or promotions, production and engineering on new product or service introduction, accounting on credit terms and customer payment issues, and other departments as needed. The telephone sales department always seems to live in the present with statements such as, "I just talked to a customer," "I need the product code now," or "She is demanding I call her back right away with an answer." Other departments may be much more future-oriented (marketing) or past-oriented (accounting).

These time horizon differences may be jarring at times. The sales manager who walks into the typical marketing department and needs something today, preferably before noon, may be shocked to find they are all working on projects with due dates weeks or months away. The sales manager who walks into accounting about a large customer that needs to temporarily go over their credit limit to place a large order may be disappointed to find out the accountants are much more focused on closing the past month. Futurologists and historians may not play well in the corporate playpen with the sales group focused on what just happened.

The sales manager must also occasionally do some organizational damage control. In my experience, telephone salespeople can be an emotional bunch at times. Partially because they expend so much emotional labor to do their jobs, partially because of the type of personalities that work well in the telephone sales job, and entirely because they are in the uncomfortable boundary position between the customer and the organization. If something doesn't go as planned, they are the sounding board on which customers take out their frustrations.

Occasionally, these frustrations are transmitted outside the sales department more aggressively and less diplomatically than the sales manager would have hoped. This produces a difficult balancing act — the sales manager must support their salespeople or see a drop-off in sales team morale, but the sales manager must also keep the salespeople from becoming pariahs within their own company.

This will be beneficial for neither the customers, who need advocates, nor the salespeople who need the organization to react when necessary. It will also be detrimental for the sales manager, who after all, has his or her own career to protect and revenue goals to deliver. The skills of an experienced diplomat are required.

Beyond the diplomacy lie the structural issues of establishing the business model, defining territories, activities, and results for each salesperson, and developing and communicating policies. Once the business model is established, the sales manager can focus on the structural issue of creating territories. This is a big decision, and customer inputs, geography, service and product issues, and a fair balance between salespeople must be considered.

If new customers are routinely flowing into the territories, the sales manager will probably want to establish territories that are easy for customer service or marketing to assign—for example, by ZIP code, telephone prefix, or state. If state regulations or boundaries imposed upon the selling organization are important, geography may be critical.

If the selling organization has service centers, depots, or drop boxes for customers, perhaps it makes sense to organize territories around these. Your organization may have unique and special requirements that influence the creation of territories.

The overall composition of these territories will influence the activity and results targets for the salesperson that ends up in each territory. For example, a mature territory with well-developed customers may require fewer phone calls but more talk time. A territory that requires a great deal of business development and prospecting may dictate less phone time, but more phone calls.

Developing and communicating policies requires an understanding of what can be done routinely and what needs to go to the sales manager. The more work product required to go to the sales manager, the less time the sales manager will have for planning, coaching, selection, and orientation. Nothing impacts the day-to-day life of the sales manager more than handling exceptions to stated policies.

What freedom does the telephone salesperson have to rectify problems? Much depends on the specific circumstances of the selling organization. In some organizations, a $100 credit can be freely given by the salesperson if need be. In another organization, this may be way too much. In others, it may be way too small. As consumers, almost all of us have been put on hold by a customer service representative while they hunted for a manager to approve some request we've made. This is the same issue the business-to-business sales manager faces.

Determine what the telephone sales reps do without your guidance through clear policies and procedures. Avoid being the adrenalin-junkie sales manager who requires their reps to come to them for everything. Rather, work hard to find the right balance, empowering your sales reps while giving them guidance.

Leading

I chose to hold our sales meetings each Friday. It was our slowest day of the week; customers were bailing out early to get a start on the weekend and the telephone sales representatives were tired and cranky after a long week. Marketing had new promotions, copy, and artwork to share. Accounting had a few policies they wanted to update. Production wanted to stick their head in and talk about a new product they had coming out in a few weeks. Fulfillment had a new shipping charge table everyone needed to begin using. And maintenance wanted to swing by and talk about next week, because they were doing an overlay on the parking lot and it would impact where people could park while construction was going on.

As I sat in my office, looking at this agenda, I thought, "this is not a sales meeting, but a communication meeting." I pictured how our usual meeting progressed — each sales rep sitting in their chair in gentle boredom, fidgeting with their smart phones, aimlessly scratching a few words on a note pad, perhaps cracking a joke at times to liven up the leaden atmosphere in the room.

Sometimes this joke would go to a nearby colleague — other times to the whole group. Nervous laughter would follow until enough of them glanced in my direction. The other departments didn't really like to talk to the sales team all that much. The salespeople always seemed a little annoyed and pompous. They did it because their bosses made them. I knew in their hearts they thought the sales reps were spoiled babies. They got commissions after all, and when they landed a big deal, we rang a bell and they paraded around like prima donnas after opening night.

On one afternoon we did something different. I emailed everyone and asked them to write down their communications on a piece of paper and make 28 copies, enough for the whole team. I asked them to be prepared to have a workshop. I emailed the sales team, "Bring a reference story to the sales meeting today and be prepared to tell it." I went to the offices of my best representatives and told them I wanted to start by having them tell us their stories, to get the conversation started. They nodded quickly, as high performers do, not seeming to think much about it. They already knew what to talk about.

People filed in nervously that afternoon. What in the world did the Vice President of Marketing and Sales have on his mind today? It was a Friday afternoon. I'm sure they were wondering, "Can't we just communicate and all get out of here?" I started off by saying we'd pass out all the communications items at the end of the meeting. I expected everyone to read them by the time they went home. There would be a quiz on Monday (barely perceptible groans and smirks), but today I wanted to do something different — accounting, marketing, maintenance, fulfillment. "Today," I said, "we will listen to customers."

I asked, "Nile, what are you hearing?"

Our best representative told a reference story. Marketing had a question. How did that customer come to us? The answer was, "From a catalog sent to a third-party list." Had she heard of us before she got the catalog? No, she thought she saw us at the annual American Society of Training and Development conference (now ATD), but she wasn't sure.

Accounting jumped in and asked why they were having problems with their teams. Nile replied, "Because of the diversity of their groups, so many cultures, and so many geographies."

"So how could we reach more people like her?" said a person from the Art Department to a copywriter who turned to the list person from marketing. It sounded like we were just lucky she got a catalog this time, and was interested enough to page through it and then pick up the phone. Luckily, customer service put her through to Nile and he could diagnose her needs.

The meeting went on like this for over an hour. And when we were done, it was the best meeting we'd had in quite some time, primarily because it was about customers. But it also opened the eyes of everyone in the room to the complexities of generating interest, of diagnosing a real-live business issue, tying it to one of our products or services, and gently guiding a customer toward a purchase.

There were multiple steps, the buying committees, and the risks of something going wrong in the customer's initiative. The customer didn't care much about our freight policies. They'd never see the parking lot, but they reached out to us with an issue. And through careful guidance, together we solved it — using the stuff we made, marketed, accounted for, and sold. That day, I taught myself something about leadership. As I said in the introduction, experience is the best teacher, although she is the most expensive.

Leadership is primarily about motivation. High-performing sales organizations are not just managed. They are led. Of course, no one person can motivate another. Each person must choose to invest energy and enthusiasm into his or her job. A well-led sales organization, however, is somewhat self-policing. Strong leadership creates a motivational culture where telephone sales representatives hold themselves accountable to a high level of performance.

The sales manager has a series of tools available to assist with establishing a motivational culture. Sales meetings are motivational because they reinforce team behavior and peer group expectations. Sales meetings also provide a great opportunity for reward and recognition activities. Managers are encouraged to establish a mechanism so the telephone sales representatives can be recognized by others within the selling organization.

Achieving a personal-best month, closing a large sale, or receiving a customer compliment can all be recognized. The telephone sales position, often an entry-level position, will not have the glamour and glory of a field sales position. However, the need for recognition may be higher, because the sales egos of the individuals involved are just being established. Any good sales culture should include leadership activities and processes that are designed to provide emotional nutrition for the telephone salesperson. Picking up the phone dozens of times a day is not an easy way to make a living; the emotional labor is taxing.

Constructing a sales culture that boosts motivation is difficult, but well worth the reward. A famous Marine once said that taking a hill under enemy fire is not just proof of patriotism or valor, but proof of the human desire to not let buddies down who are also charging up the hill. So too does a high-performing sales culture boost motivation by setting the bar high and expecting everyone to clear it — each and every day.

Sales Culture

A sales culture can be defined as the collective mindsets of its members. Mindsets are how people see the world. They reflect a set of beliefs formed through experience. The mindsets of salespeople determine how they filter and interpret their sales world. This influences their decision-making processes and their behavior.

Almost every sales organization has stories and informal conversations that shape the mindsets of its members and create the culture. The sales manager can influence the establishment of this culture by working on the areas they can influence. They can't directly influence the informal "water cooler" conversations, but the sales manager can influence much of what takes place within the walls of the selling organization.

The sales culture, more than anything, tells a new telephone sales representative what is expected. If high expectations are documented and presented in Personal Business Plans, but the everyday actions of the salesperson's peers do not reflect these expectations, the new telephone sales rep will probably settle at the level of the rest of the group. The basic tools of the sales manager revolve around storytelling, meetings, conversations, coaching, and apprenticeship.

Sales Meetings

Many sales organizations hold weekly meetings to discuss new products and services, organizational issues, goals, and objectives. Sales meetings can be powerful tools to also build the mindsets that form the sales culture. Games and activities can be used in sales meetings to reinforce sales concepts and let the group engage in a spirited joint activity. As I indicated when starting this section, the sales manager shouldn't let the sales meeting turn just into a communications meeting; share stories and promote dialogue with other departments.

Sales Contests

Sales contests can also boost a culture by spurring friendly competition and providing motivation. Contests don't need to be about money; they can be for a couple hours of time off, the cubicle closest to the restroom, or a banner that says, "Number One." And don't think competitions need to be about the individual. Team contests in a large sales group can also be motivational. At one place where I worked as a sales manager, we had a professional dress code — shirts and ties for the guys. I started a sales contest where the winner could wear anything that was casually appropriate. (In other words, no beach apparel.)

It worked better than money. Another time when I was a vice president of sales, we did a "Gold Rush" and the sales manager dressed up as a 49er, complete with dollar bills hanging out of his pockets. We gave out $50 and $100 bills on the spot for various contest objectives (and then quickly told the accounting department for tax purposes). Be creative. (See Document 17-10 at BPGrp.com on Sales Contest Ideas.)

Career Path

Many selling organizations decide to use the telephone selling group as a "farm team" for other sales, management, and marketing positions. In this case, the career path for a new telephone sales representative was established and set at the time of hire. Other organizations adopt a "wait-and-see" approach. For these firms, the telephone sales representative may apply for other positions once he or she is qualified, but a career path is not mapped out at the time of hire. Whatever selection sales management makes, it's important to communicate the career paths open to salespeople, as future possibilities are motivational.

Many selling organizations will hire a telephone sales representative who aspires to be nothing but the best rep possible. There are telephone salespeople in organizations I've consulted with who've been in the job for 20 years! This path — the one to technical sales excellence — is a path you should consider if you find an individual who likes selling over the phone as a destination position.

These long-term salespeople provide true bench strength for the sales manager. They are successful (or they would have moved on a long time ago) and they are often capable mentors with the ability and drive to take new telephone salespeople under their wings. A good mentoring program can serve not only the experienced telephone sales representative, but also the sales manager.

Rewards and Recognition

Rewards and recognition are critical to a sales organization. After all, there is no other part of the business that hears "no" more often than the sales group. Rewards such as a "personal-best month" certificate can be relatively simple. Consider giving out rewards on a quarterly or monthly basis by recognizing such things as:

- "Personal Best" — When a telephone salesperson sells more in a month than he or she sold in any previous month.
- "Highest Sales" — For a period of time.
- "Two Million Dollar Club" — For achieving a certain level of sales (it need not be $2 million) in the last 12 months. Perhaps the salesperson gets his or her portrait up on the wall in the sales department.
- "Salesperson of the Year" — For a defined customer-centric metric such as "satisfaction," "account growth," etc.
- "Hardest Working" – highest number of dials or phone time in a quarter.
- "Most Improved" — Largest increase in sales in an established territory.
- "Early Bird" — First to sell a brand-new product or service.
- "Gold Rush Champ" — Highest sales during a sales contest.

The recognition a salesperson receives from his or her manager is perhaps the most important. Your salespeople are in a boundary position at the selling organization — with one foot planted in the customer's business and one foot inside the organization. This boundary position causes considerable tension for the salesperson on an ongoing basis, and recognition provides emotional nutrition for the telephone representative to go back and do the job all over again.

Compensation

I always debate with myself on whether compensation is a management task or a leadership task. I typically bend toward leadership, because the compensation plan should be motivational. The selling organization may decide to provide at-risk compensation based on performance, or may not. I've consulted with organizations that pay a straight base salary. I've worked with others who transition the telephone sales rep to 100%

commission after providing a draw when they start. The sales manager, in consultation with senior management, will need to decide what is best for the selling organization. There is no one rule of thumb. If at-risk pay is offered, the primary consideration is the influence the telephone salesperson has over what is being compensated.

If they have little influence, the compensation plan will be demotivational. It they have a great deal of influence, it will be motivational. I favor at-risk pay at some level. At-risk pay rewards the telephone salesperson for the emotional labor invested in the job. It is the return they bring home and a source of pride. (See Document 17-11 at BPGrp.com on Compensation Plan ideas.)

Chapter 18
The Great Recession: Journey to a Billion

Don't all good business plans start on a cocktail napkin?

On Friday, June 22, 2012, Mark and I were sitting in the bar of the Langham Hotel in Melbourne, Australia. The Langham sits on the banks of the Yarra River. It is a short walk to the Royal Botanic Gardens, which contain thousands of plants unlike anything you see in the United States. The Yarra itself is always full of small crew boats with rowers facing backward dashing up or down the river, being guided by a coach with a bull horn riding a bike down one side of the river.

The Langham is also a short walk from the MCG, the Melbourne Cricket Grounds where Australian Football League games are held, and the Rod Laver Arena where the Australian Open is played, which is part of the tennis Grand Slam. At the foot of the bridge where I went back across the Yarra stood the Victoria Bitter brewery, called by the locals simply VB.

Mark and I were relaxing after finishing five days of training for the ISRs of the Australian dealers. We ordered a martini, and began a long discussion of the state of the telephone sales program and where it was going at Caterpillar. We agreed dealers were adopting the telephone selling platform globally, that hundreds of millions of dollars of incremental revenue was being generated, and that scores of new ISRs were being hired each quarter.

Mark asked me, "What would it take to hit a billion dollars of incremental revenue?" Moments later, the waitress came by and asked, "Would you guys like another round?" We said we would and I asked for a few extra napkins.

I began doing some quick math. We had about 350 ISRs working globally at the time, and using the incremental revenue we should be able to generate, I said, "Mark, it looks like we'd be able to hit a billion in 2017. We'd need to be at about 1,000 ISRs globally by then. The math is a little complicated, because as new positions are added, they take three years to get up to a full run rate." Quickly the next napkin had various slopes and assumptions written on it. "So, what work would we have to do at a corporate level to make that happen?" Mark said, half to himself and half to me. Quickly I grabbed a third napkin and we began to do an abbreviated SWOT analysis (Strengths, Weaknesses, Opportunities, Threats).

"Here are your drinks guys," the waitress said. She looked down and asked, "Do you need more napkins?"

I said, "Sure," and asked for a couple more.

The strengths included our global brand leadership. Since we just finished three days of listening to ISRs call customers at our training session, we both thought we had extremely receptive customers — eager to build a relationship with their local dealer. On one call, I recalled the ISR had a customer say he hadn't heard from us for five years since he last bought a machine, but was delighted we'd reached out.

Others this week immediately asked "if they owed any money" when the ISR identified themselves as calling from the dealership. They assumed the ISR was calling to collect money … not build a relationship, not see what their business needed from us to grow. We agreed the dealer network was a strength. They know their local communities and could adapt the ISR program to local conditions. We also had a seven-year track record to build upon, with implementation guidebooks and training programs in place for both sales managers and salespeople.

What about weaknesses? We didn't have all the material translated in major languages yet. And we didn't have instructors in languages in all the jurisdictions. We would need to use our three-pronged implementation strategy of dealer exchanges, implementation guidebooks, and sales manager training more aggressively and in language. We also had cultural differences to overcome in many places. This had especially been true in China where there was a reluctance to do business over the phone. And then Mark reminded me that a weakness was that he was a team of one. Managing the program at its current size was already more than a full-time job; the time commitment would grow along with the size of the program.

What was our opportunity? When the Great Recession began to bite in early 2009, many dealers were forced to lay off employees. Because ISRs were recent hires, many were caught up in the layoffs even though they were in revenue-generating positions. Our census of in-place ISRs fell by 40% as the recession began to bite.

But China reacted to the Great Recession by aggressively pursuing public work projects, and other nations began to ramp up infrastructure projects to stimulate their economies. The resulting commodity boom strongly increased demand for heavy equipment, parts, and service. This resulted in a quick recovery in ISR numbers as the dealer network returned to profitability. Our opportunity, Mark and I agreed, was to keep this acceleration going until we hit a billion.

Threats? Mark said he thought the biggest threat was the lack of managers trained to support open-dialogue telephone selling. Field salespeople at the time still outnumbered telephone salespeople by three to one. Most managers were experienced in field sales, not telephone sales. This had been a real struggle for us historically, and if the accelerated pace continued, it would only get worse. Mark was also worried about the two political issues.

First, as the initiative grew, he would have to sell everything to multiple other managers within the organization and this was always hard. Every manager had their own set of priorities, and Mark needed to make sure that striving for a billion complemented where each manager was invested. Second, at the dealer level, dealers didn't like anything "cooked up in the Caterpillar kitchen." Dealers sometimes had a love/hate relationship with the mother ship. They obviously loved the product, but didn't like corporations to be overbearing or too directive. Since our goal was to keep an accelerated schedule of hiring and training, we'd need to be careful to support the dealers, not tell them what to do.

"Would you like another?" the waitress asked. "No", we replied almost in unison. Two is plenty.

As we left the bar, I turned to Mark, clutching the napkins, and asked, "What should we call this rapid growth initiative?"

"March to a billion," said Mark.

I leaned over and wrote it on the top of the first napkin. That night I couldn't sleep, and so early in the morning I began working on an Excel spreadsheet showing how many ISRs we would need — and when — to hit Mark's goal. At breakfast, it was all we could talk about.

We were back in the United States for only a few days when we met with Mark's new boss's boss, Kirk. Bob Morrison had taken the early retirement package offered when the recession was at its worst. Kirk strongly encouraged us to go for it. From his perspective, the ISR initiative fit into the "life cycle of coverage" program he was developing. Low potential accounts would be covered by marketing, smaller customers by inside sales representatives (telephone selling), and larger customers by field sales.

He encouraged us to look at trends. Was the number of smaller customers growing? What was the impact on dealers because we had such fast turnover in ISRs? ISRs were turning over, because dealers were using the ISR program as a "first sales job" within the dealership and were quickly promoting them to field sales and managerial positions. We had ISRs that went through sales training, and within weeks were promoted. Good for them, good for the dealership, but a tough demand on the ISR program.

We talked about "taking managers to the next level." Kirk asked, "So, after you give them the initial training (our customized Leading High-Impact Sales program), what's next?" Going to the white board in his corner office, he wrote "Life Cycle." We need to focus on the ISRs part of this "Condition Monitoring" because we need to promote ways to foster equipment health. He also wrote "Coverage" to cover accounts that aren't being covered. Underneath these words, he wrote "Burning Platforms."

"Connect these dots," he said. "Address these burning platforms." He circled each. As we got up to leave, Kirk said, "I don't like your name, 'March to a Billion.' It sounds too military. How about, Journey?"

"Journey to a Billion" was born.

Mark and I went to his office right afterwards, and Mark told me his biggest concern was getting the other managers internally who were involved in Kirk's other initiatives to back the ISR "Journey." If they saw "Journey to a Billion" as competitive, or able to steal resources or monopolize dealer attention, it would be politically difficult to garner their support.

He also reasoned that if these other managers from Caterpillar sang the praises of the ISR "Journey" to dealers tangential to their own initiatives, the "Journey" wouldn't sound like it was cooked up in the "Caterpillar kitchen." Rather, it would seem like "Journey" was spreading organically, dealer to dealer, and these other Caterpillar managers were like bees flying flower to flower, dropping a little pollen where ever they went.

So, our message to these managers would be, "The dealers are on a 'Journey to a Billion' of incremental revenue using telephone salespeople. We call them ISRs. We think ISRs can help sell what you're working on. Tell us about it. We may be able to incorporate it into our training programs." Politically clever and astute I thought. The message these other Caterpillar managers would say to the dealers would be, "We know you dealers are on a 'Journey to Billion' of incremental revenue using telephone sales. We have something that will sell like hotcakes to their customers." Great messaging.

On July 12th, we met with the coverage team. They were working to make sure all customers had the appropriate sales and marketing contact. They had several initiatives to broaden sales contacts to smaller customers and the telephone sales program seemed like a great fit. Mark discussed the dealer initiative "Journey to a Billion," and how he was "helping" support the initiative from a corporate level. Their team would recommend dealers look at implementing telephone sales for smaller customers and this would help the team achieve their goals.

Later that afternoon, we met with the Lifecycle team. They had recently conducted interviews with large and small contractors with older machines trying to define a strategy to effectively cover these customers.

They had also done a study of other businesses in this space to look at loyalty programs and the value story they were taking to the marketplace. They talked to us about how telephone sales representatives (ISRs) could help gather information on customer's email addresses and find out information on their fleet. They would recommend dealers implement telephone sales. I was already working with the "Condition Monitoring" people on another initiative, so I began planting the "Journey to a Billion" seeds with them.

On July 19th, we met with Kirk again, and we discussed our thought that we needed to develop another sales manager workshop to take them to the next level. We had "Leading High-Impact Sales" for new managers, but we needed something for managers striving to reach the next level. I suggested we call it "Advanced Telephone Selling," but Kirk thought that sounded flat and mushy.

"How about 'Performance Breakthrough Workshop?'" he asked.

Great name. That's why he gets paid the big bucks.

Mark and I began to look closely at how dealers were deploying telephone sales (ISRs). We had a contingent selling product support (parts and service) for machines, which is where we started. We had other ISRs selling product support for power systems — mainly standby generators. Yet others were selling machines over the phone — mainly smaller machines like skid steers. Mark was contacted by business units in Marine and Oil and Gas. Could ISRs be deployed to help them? We began thinking about how we could customize the iron triangle of dealer exchanges, implementation guidebooks, and training for each of these specialties.

This journey was getting complicated.

Chapter 19
CLOSE: Overcoming Objections

"Objection!" yelled the defense attorney, jumping to her feet.

As the prosecutor turned with a smug expression on his face, the defense lawyer addressed the judge. "Your honor, this is strictly hearsay! It's totally inadmissible."

The prosecutor turned slowly toward the bench. He mused to himself, "Well the jury heard the witness say it, didn't they? It will be impossible for them to forget." He paced deliberately in front of the jury. Turning his head slightly, he noticed the jurors looked shocked, mouths agape — everyone at rapt attention.

"Sustained!" ruled the judge. "The jury will overlook what the witness just said."

"Victory!" crowed the prosecutor to himself, silently meeting the glance of his admiring colleagues.

Okay, perhaps a sales objection doesn't have the emotional punch of a crowded courtroom, but to the telephone salesperson, an objection is a supreme court challenge. How do humans express displeasure first? Typically, with body language. Objections are conflict, and most people would rather not directly confront someone verbally if they can express their displeasure in another way. People usually begin their communication with body language. What's next in the communication menu? Tone of voice. The edge begins to show. The words are short and choppy. Irritation enters the tone. What's last? Word choice. "Your price is too high!"

Unfortunately for the telephone salesperson, they can't see the customer, so body language is not communicated, and they and the customer may only have one ear in the game using a cell phone, handset, or one-sided headset, and tone of voice is much harder to pick up than if they were face-to-face. Nevertheless, since body language and tone of voice are mostly instinctual, the customer may feel they've communicated their displeasure, but the telephone salesperson had little chance of picking up these valuable clues. When the objection is finally communicated verbally, it's real and it must be overcome immediately.

If you're selling a product or service that has high value, and a higher price than the competition, you can expect a price objection. The best way to handle a price objection is to prepare for it. The best ammunition comes from the needs analysis. It could be, "You told me you were looking for the lowest cost per hour. The initial investment in our solution may be a little higher, but the operating costs will be lower and the resale value much higher. This leads to a lower cost per hour over your expected usage. Do you want to review the numbers again?"

Customers go to purchasing school just like salespeople go to sales training. Customers have been taught to object to prices to see if they are getting the best deal. In this example, the salesperson established the parameters as "lowest cost per hour" during the needs analysis, which provides the best way to defend the selling organization's value.

With high-value products or services, positioning during the sales conversation is important. In the example above, "lowest cost per hour" can be used to complete on price, even though the original investment may be higher. During the needs analysis, it is likely the customer will articulate "the best price" as one of their requirements. It may be put another way like "fits within my budget" or "lowest-cost investment."

The telephone salesperson can help the customer define this as "lowest cost per hour" and will then be prepared for the price objection. In other cases, the positioning selected may be higher. In this case, the salesperson must uncover needs which competitors can't address and use these to overcome the price objection. This "my product or service is an apple; their product or service is an orange" is a valuable benefit of proper positioning.

Another tactic to address a price objection is to create steps in the sales process that build the perception of value or uniqueness. For example, we have a client who sells medical devices which are used by orthopedic surgeons in joints such as shoulders, knees, and hips. The client has a mobile lab where surgeons can "saw bones" and try their products out in a laboratory setting. The sales representative can recommend this step as part of the sales cycle. "Before making a decision, many of my clients ask us to send over our mobile lab. You can try out our products in a laboratory setting, and prove to yourself how our products will save you time in the operating room and improve customer satisfaction."

Offering this step helps even if the customer does not take you up on this step in the sales cycle. One of the steps I always offer new clients in our sales cycles is to contact existing clients for a reference. Mark Wankel from Caterpillar has been on my reference list for over a decade, and I think only two people have ever called him. Customers assume that if you offer the step, it must be in your favor, so it is impressive even if they never take you up on it. Obviously, some customers will, so the step needs to be legitimate.

Consider what steps you may add to the sales process to head off objections before they occur, or if they do, to provide ammunition for the salesperson to use in their response. These steps may be plant tours, references, third-party verification such as ISO 9000, or case studies with facts and figures. I have another client who sells hardware with a higher tensile strength than the competition. If he can get a customer to visit the plant, they pull apart a bolt. The potential customers will watch as the pulling strength gets higher and higher and then bang! The bolt breaks with a huge snap. It's always impressive. For those that can't visit, a video does the same task, although less dramatically than in person.

Additional steps in the sales cycle can address other issues besides price. When the telephone salesperson uncovers the buying committee, and ascertains their needs, they may uncover additional steps to add for these individuals. For example, the salesperson may uncover all purchase orders needed to run by the CFO prior to signature. The salesperson should call the accounting department, and find out what processes and procedures, hoops and hurdles new vendors are required to jump through and add those to the sales cycle. If possible, the salesperson should get these tasks completed and should tell their contact before asking for the sale. Knock away the potential objection before it occurs.

When I was a sales manager, during our sales meetings, I'd always ask the group to tell me about any objections they heard the previous week. To groans and arm-waving disgruntlement, I'd uncover the product and price road blocks which came our way. Then I'd say, "What could we ask during needs analysis to provide ammunition to overcome this objection or what steps could we add to the sales cycle?" My goal every week was to get better as a department.

Sales is a process. A sale is an event. The sales manager should study how to position their product or service, what questions need to be asked during the needs analysis, and what additional steps in the sales cycle may be incorporated to overcome objections. Once this is done, the manager should train the salespeople accordingly, because objections will come.

So, what does the salesperson say when an objection occurs? We teach a three-step process called ACT. Acknowledge, Clarify and respond, and Transition back to the sales process. The first step is to acknowledge, and the goal is to let the customer know you have heard him or her without reinforcing the objection. For example, if the customer says, "Your price is too high," a response may be, "I understand value is important to you." The salesperson needs to be careful not to reinforce the objection during the acknowledgement. In the example above, "Yes, it's pretty expensive, isn't it?" would be a poor response.

The second step is to Clarify and then respond. The salesperson may need to ask, "What are you comparing my quote to," or "What about the mowing deck was a concern to you," or additional questions which uncover the essence of the objection. The response should come from the proper needs analysis the telephone salesperson did when the need was originally uncovered. Again, examples include, "You told me a warranty was important to you," or "you told me a mower deck which rode over uneven ground was a critical concern to you." The best response comes from needs the customer articulated early in the sales process.

The Transition step is to tie the objection in a knot and move on. "Have I addressed your concern?" or "Does this make sense to you?" These are basically trial closes that tell the salesperson they have answered the customer's objection and it is time to move on, probably to closing the sale.

A special type of objection is the stall. This is where the telephone salesperson never gets a "yes" or a "no," but the sales cycle just sort of grinds to a slow halt, and no firm decision is ever made. Earlier in the book, you learned about adding steps in the sales cycle to avoid a stall, and the importance of creating a timeline. Stalls can also occur as objections in business-to-business, most commonly statements like, "I have to run this by my boss," or other buying committee objections.

The telephone salesperson should try to cut as many of these as he or she can off at the pass, by doing a good job of probing for the buying committee and their needs. When these objections occur at the end of the sales cycle, the salesperson should instantly realize they really aren't done selling. An acknowledgement like,"I understand your boss must be consulted," can be followed up with a clarification such as, "Tell me what criteria your boss will use to evaluate the solution you and I have crafted." At this point, the salesperson's contact should be on the team to help close the sale. But the real decision maker is the boss.

During our telephone salesperson training classes, we outline typical objections and brainstorm items such as acknowledgements, clarifications, responses, and transitions, along with steps we could have added to the sales cycle, and questions we could have asked. The focus should be on avoiding objections, but if they do occur, we discuss how to address them for maximum success.

A lawyer friend of mine once told me that you never ask a question in open court if you don't already know the answer. So, in a way, the sales objection is like the court room objection. Always ask questions early that provide answers to later objections, and look for evidence you can add to build up your sales cycles. If necessary, address the objection calmly and ACT. Doing this, the salesperson can tell the story at the next sales meeting of how they calmly overcame a sticky objection, and crow to themselves as they silently meet the glance of their admiring colleagues.

Chapter 20
Atten Hut! The Boot Camp Era Begins

At the depths of the Great Recession, our staff at Business Performance Group began meeting with Mark and other members of his team each December to plan the upcoming year. We'd discuss our growth targets, and all the tasks that needed to be completed to meet the objectives.

By the fall of 2010, Bill Buss had retired from Finning Canada and joined Business Performance Group as a senior consultant. To broaden the sales training experience, we had tested the concept of a "Boot Camp," which would include our training session, and several days on the phone making calls with a coach listening in. The goal was to cement the sales concepts into behaviors before releasing the telephone salespeople back into their dealerships.

Our first Boot Camp was in Edmonton when Bill was still working there. I conducted the training session, and Bill did the coaching afterwards. The results were impressive. The techniques were driven home by practice, and the reps were confident. I conducted follow-up Boot Camps in Birmingham, Alabama, and Novi, Michigan, in the fall of 2010. As Bill and I were preparing for our annual meeting with Mark, we came up with the idea of sponsoring Boot Camps in our facility for dealers across the country. We'd go through the training session and then put them on the phone. After a few days of coaching, we'd take them to Peoria for additional product training. We'd create a list of online courses to complete as pre-requisites, and specify an expected time between hire and Boot Camp to assure the reps had gone through their orientation.

In December of 2010 we proposed this to Mark. He was a little skeptical the dealers would send their people to a 10-day training session, or bear the cost, but he gave us the go-ahead to try. Our first Boot Camp rolled out in May of 2011 and we initially planned on doing three or four a year. By the time the "Journey to a Billion" was hatched, we were holding 10 per year, plus several internationally, including the "Boot Camp" in Melbourne, Australia, where Mark and I came up with the idea for the "Journey."

The iron triangle of implementation for the "Journey to a Billion" was the dealer exchanges, implementation guidebooks, and training courses. As the number of ISRs was growing globally, we realized that telephone sales were now being used for product support for machines where it started, as well as machine sales, power systems, oil and gas, marine, and product support of larger machines we called "core." To be successful, we recognized we needed to specialize.

We created implementation guidebooks for each of these uses of telephone selling, and we also began offering specialized Boot Camps. This included a workshop in Hamburg, Germany, for the division of Caterpillar that created engines for seagoing vessels. Domestically, we launched separate Boot Camps for power systems, machine sales, and product support for machine.

To service ISRs internationally, we began recruiting presenters at Business Performance Group who could teach in language. This included Russian, Japanese, French, Mandarin, Bahasa (Indonesia), and South African English.

The Russian instructor we recruited was Svetlana Smirnova. We invited her to the United States where she attended one of our Boot Camps, and on August 31, 2012, we traveled to Russia to participate in her first Boot Camp in country after we had translated our materials. At first, Mark and I almost didn't get to go. We learned Russia restricted travel to the cities listed on the visa you acquired. Our visas listed Moscow and St. Petersburg, but after we received our visas, the local dealer moved the Boot Camp to Nizhny Novgorod (formerly the Soviet City of Gorky). After a few days of scrambling to see what we should do, I finally placed a call to the U.S. Embassy in Moscow, and they assured us that since our arrival and departure destinations were correct, we would be okay.

We landed in Moscow and took the train to Nizhny located on the Volga. On the way, we sat in a train compartment that looked like something out of the Orient Express, complete with vodka brought to us in tiny containers. In Nizhny, we walked down to the banks of the Volga every day, and took a small boat across to the other shore where the dealer would pick us up. The class was in Russian, so Mark and I sat in the back and fielded questions from Svetlana in English if one arose. The conversation was often animated, with 11 students arranged around a horseshoe-shaped table. After two days in the classroom, we arranged phones around the table and called customers. Earlier, I had trained their managers on how to coach. Svetlana also provided coaching and the excitement of the day occurred when a new telephone sales representative sold a skid steer.

Later that night, we had a dinner with the dealer at a local restaurant, and rather than taking the boat, the dealer drove us back the long way to a bridge across the Volga on another side of town. As we approached our hotel, we noticed the always-busy parking lot was almost empty, and two imposing men in black suits were standing near the front door. As we pulled up, one of the men approached the door and talked excitedly in Russian. Our escort told us to get out of the car and go straight to our rooms, which we did, locking the doors behind us. This ended our brief encounter with the Russian underworld.

On Friday, we left Nizhny via the high-speed train back to Moscow. As we arrived at the train station, Svetlana didn't see the sign for the train, so she asked Mark and me to wait in the waiting room. Nothing was in English. When Nizhny was Gorky, it was closed to westerners, and few knew any English and neither of us knew any Russian. As the minutes passed, Mark and I remarked that if Svetlana didn't return, we would be waiting in the train station probably forever. When she did return, she motioned us to quickly follow which we did, overjoyed she came back for us, dodging around platforms, climbing and descending stairs until we reached the platform that said "Mockba" (Russian for Moscow).

The next morning, we headed back home, leaving the Marriott Royal Aurora Hotel near Red Square, arriving at the airport at 3:30 a.m. The terminal was jam packed, and you needed to go through security twice, first just to get into the terminal, and second when you traveled to your gate. Once inside the terminal, nothing was in English; everything was in Russian and we walked helplessly until a kind British Airways flight attendant pointed us in the right direction. Once in line at the Lufthansa counter, we were told since we had bags to check, we needed to go over into a second line and pay the fee for our luggage. They gave me my tickets, but the agent kept Mark's. After enduring the second line, we went back to get Mark's ticket, only to find the agent was gone and no one else could understand what we were looking for, given our German and Russian were limited. After many anxious minutes, the tickets were located behind the counter and off we went to the second security line and customs.

Mark went through customs first, and the gal behind the counter, looking grim and stern in her military uniform, gave his papers, passport, and visa a cursory glance. When I went up to the line, she began carefully reviewing every page. She typed into her computer and stared at the response. She looked at my passport again, and typed again. More looking at the screen. Meanwhile, Mark was waiting behind the counter for me to come through, and both of us were getting more and more concerned. After what seemed like an eternity, but was only about four minutes, she stamped my passport, handed everything back to me, and motioned me through. I have no idea to this day what that was all about.

We also had international Boot Camps in Australia as I've mentioned before, and in China, Egypt, South Africa, Britain, France, Germany, Singapore, Algeria, Dubai, Chile, Panama, Argentina, Canada, and a few places I've probably forgotten to mention. We also trained instructors for sessions in Indonesia, India, and Japan. We learned our telephone selling technique is more universal than we first thought, we learned that businesses globally want to succeed and treasure suppliers who share their vision.

We learned that face-to-face selling is expensive almost everywhere, and the worldwide explosion and use of the smart phone has enabled the telephone sales representative to compete on a global scale. As I mentioned in the chapter on relationships, sometimes everything didn't translate smoothly, but in the end, we found the language of business is universal.

Chapter 21
CLOSE: The Brush Off

I usually buy my clothes online, but on a Saturday not long ago, I found myself in a store looking for a new shirt. I was staring intently at a row of dress shirts when a sales clerk came up to me on my right-hand side and said, "Can I help you?"

I barely turned to her as I continued to look at the rows of shirts and I said, "No thanks. Just looking." As she walked away, I looked up from the shirts and thought to myself, "Well, I could have used some help, I guess." I gave her the brush off.

The "brush off" is a lack of interest objection, and it is such a special objection it deserves its own chapter. Earlier we focused on the compelling reason to call, which is the way to overcome the human brain's tendency to continue what it is already doing. But what if that doesn't work? What if the customer cuts off the telephone salesperson before they even launch into their compelling reason to call? They've been brushed off.

"Just send me something."
"We don't have any needs right now."
"I'll call you if I need you."
"We're happy with our current supplier."

The telephone salesperson should have a call outline in front of them with great open-ended questions to prompt a good conversation. They should have excellent closed-ended questions to uncover facts, which will help them determine whether there is a potential win-win situation. How can they get the three to four minutes it will take?

The same format can be used as with any other objection: Acknowledge, Clarify and respond, and Transition back to the sales process. Our goal here is to overcome the brush off and get into the needs analysis. Not a lot of clarification needs to be done. There isn't much to clarify, and our response should be an interest-generating question that serves to transition us into our call outline.

Customer: "Just send me something."

Telephone Salesperson: "I'd be happy to send some information. So I can save you time and tailor what I send you to your specific needs, can I ask you a couple of quick questions?"

In this case, "I'd be happy to send some information" is our acknowledgement.. As soon as the customer hears this, they begin to relax because the telephone salesperson has acknowledged their request to send them information, and they think this distraction of a telephone call will soon end. The transition "can I ask you a couple of quick questions" sounds reasonable. What should follow is the best open-ended question the salesperson has on the call outline. This question should generate some interest, and spark some dialogue. The brush-off is quickly forgotten, and the sales conversation commences. Let's try another one:

Customer: "We don't have any needs right now."

Telephone Salesperson: "I'm glad you don't have any problems you are working on right now. Just so I can prepare to help you in the future, can I ask just a couple of questions about your business before I let you go?"

There may not be any "problems" top of mind, but there might be opportunities and strategies the telephone salesperson can uncover, if only they can get a few minutes to explore these with the customer. Remember, problems are top of mind. Opportunities and strategies lie beneath, and dialogue will uncover them. Here's another:

Customer: "I'll call you if I need you."

Telephone Salesperson: "I'd truly welcome your call. So I can prepare for your call, can I ask you a few quick questions?

It seems logical the salesperson would want to prepare for the customer's call, and almost all customers will allow a few questions. Again, the best open-ended question from the call outline would be helpful here. And another example:

Customer: "We're happy with our current supplier."

Telephone Salesperson: "I understand you have a current supplier. What do you like about the products/services you are receiving from them?"

Almost all customers will tell you what they like about their current supplier, and a great follow-up question from the telephone sales representative is, "What would you change if you could?" Between "what do you like" and "what would you change," the salesperson should know exactly how to sell to this customer.

Whatever industry you're in, whatever your telephone salespeople are selling, you will have unique brush-offs from your suspects, prospects, and customers. The sales manager should make brush-offs a topic of conversation during sales meetings, and should capture good techniques for overcoming the objections you hear. In my experience, five or six brush offs cover 80% of what telephone salespeople will hear in any specific industry. Once you have great ways of overcoming these, document them, spread them around, and train new representatives how to handle them.

A good way to coach handling brush-offs for the sales manager is to have their representatives call them internally or on their cell phone. On each call, give a typical brush-off, and listen as the telephone salesperson overcomes the objection. Continue the call long enough to assure the salesperson can transition back into the sales process. If you have five or six typical brush-offs, do the process five or six times. For new telephone salespeople, do this every day for at least five days of their orientation, preferably the five days before they get on the phone. If you do, they will be skilled at overcoming these brush-offs before their first encounter with a customer.

The chilliest call is the cold call. In this case, the telephone salesperson is handed a list of suspects (identified by demographics and hopefully psychographics) and told to make something happen. This is the hardest call of all, and will be filled with brush-offs. What to do? As a sales manager, consider what strategies you might employ.

First, as I mentioned earlier, you may want to find a department within your target organizations that will talk to you, and fill you in on who to call, and to develop a specific compelling reason to call. For example, for a hydraulic pump manufacturer client of ours, we called the quality department first to find out what issues the suspect company may be having with their current supplier or any upcoming new product development. Is there anyone you can call who will give you enough information inside to warm up the call to the decision maker?

Another possible avenue is to strictly call gatekeepers first. The telephone salesperson will explain they want to email or mail information on their firm, and to find out who the right person would be at the target organization, and this person's email or mailing address. After the gatekeeper gives the telephone salesperson that information, they can do an "oh, by the way" question to find out information about the suspect's business — information the telephone salesperson can use to customize the compelling reason to call to the decision maker. First call to the gatekeeper, second call to the decision maker after the introductory email or snail mail.

Why this two-step approach? Because, when the telephone salesperson is cold calling, the gatekeeper will be hesitant to put them through to the decision maker. The result will probably be voicemail, and the likelihood that someone will respond to a generic voicemail is low. If the salesperson can glean enough information from the gatekeeper call to craft a unique compelling reason to call from inside information, they are far better off.

Gatekeeper: "XYZ Corporation, how can I help you?"

Telephone salesperson: "Hi, my name is Anne Salesperson from Acme HVAC Services in Anytown. XYZ Corporation is on my customer list, but I don't have a contact person at your organization. I'd like to send an email to this person with my contact information so they can reach out to me if they have any problems or if there is anything I can help them with. Can you tell me who in your organization is responsible for the maintenance of your heating and air conditioning systems?"

Gatekeeper: "That would be Marvin Maintenance."

Telephone Salesperson: "Great, can you give me Marvin's email and I'll send him my contact information?"

Gatekeeper: "It's <u>M.Maintenance@XYZ.com.</u>"

Telephone Salesperson: "Thank you. *<pause>* Oh by the way, so I can make sure I get the right information to Mr. Maintenance, can you tell me a little bit about what XYZ does? It looks like in my notes like you have several office parks in the area."

The goal is to uncover enough about XYZ so the telephone salesperson can customize the email to Mr. Maintenance, and to craft a compelling reason to call from the information to call him back in a week.

Compelling Reason to Call: "Mr. Maintenance, my name is Anne Salesperson from Acme HVAC Services in Anytown. I understand you are responsible for three office parks in Anytown, and your customers include three health care providers, a GSA governmental contract and five retail businesses. My company specializes in commercial HVAC services where uptime is critical, and 24-hour response time is an absolute requirement. Tell me how you maintain your heating and air conditioning units."

Mr. Maintenance: "I'm happy with my current supplier." *<Brush-off>*

Telephone Salesperson: "I understand you have a current supplier. What do you like about the service you are receiving from them?"

Mr. Maintenance: "Well, they come when we call and they take care of the problems."

Telephone Salesperson: "If you could wave your magic wand, what would you change about your heating and air conditioning services?" *<open-ended, toss me your wish list question>*

Mr. Maintenance: *<chuckles>* "I guess I'd make it less expensive. I'm on a tight budget."

Telephone Salesperson: "Okay, you're on a tight budget." *<reflection>*

Mr. Maintenance: "Of course. Out of this budget I must take care of the snow removal, lawn care, and janitorial services. We're locked into long-term contracts, and I just don't have the opportunity to get an increase, just because an air conditioner went down."

And our telephone salesperson should know where to go from here. The critical information "you are responsible for three office parks in Anytown, and your customers include three health care providers, a GSA governmental contract and five retail businesses" came from the gatekeeper on the first call. The brush-off should be expected. It may be one of six she was prepared to address.

Some telephone salespeople spend an extensive amount of time perusing the suspect's website prior to making the call. This can be helpful, but the information you really need comes from someone on the inside. The successful representative will discipline themselves to use the publicly available information to give them a general education about the customer, but someone inside to give them the real scoop. Companies don't put their problems, opportunities, and strategies on their websites. Corporate websites are designed by the suspect's marketing department in most cases, and they aren't intended to display the suspect's internal business issues. Websites can be helpful. Conversations are critical.

When a telephone salesperson who is shadowing me catches me looking at the website of a business who may be a potential client, I quickly brush them off by saying, "I'm just looking." And then I pick up the phone and I give the suspect a call.

Chapter 22
And the Award Goes to...

When we returned from Moscow, Mark was asked by Annette Burk, a colleague of his at Caterpillar, to apply for the 2012 "Chairman's Process Sustainability Award." Mark was cautious at first, given the amount of work required to pull together the submission, but Annette was persistent and talented, and together they entered the Inside Sales Representative Growth Program. The first part of the competition was to construct a booth showing the facts and figures. Senior management then toured, visiting each booth in succession, and talking to the managers tending the display. The senior managers also took a great deal of notes.

The ISR program made it to the semifinals, and I was invited to attend the final ceremony where the winner and other finishers were announced. The ISR program came in second, just behind a project to re-power the D11, which is the largest bulldozer that Caterpillar makes. As Mark said, "You can't get in the way of a D11!" And of course in a product company, it's nearly impossible for a dealer sales initiative to beat out a huge product development. Out of the hundreds of initial entries, we were delighted to come in second.

As 2013 dawned, the second-place finish in the Chairman's Award and the launch of "Journey to a Billion" created a lot of activity. In March, we piloted the Performance Breakthrough workshop for experienced dealer managers, and held a dealer exchange for domestic dealers. In April, Svetlana, our Russian language facilitator, and I facilitated an ISR and ISR Manager Course in Malaga, Spain. I conducted the manager course in parallel with Svetlana training the ISRs. At the end of the training session, we put the salespeople on the phone and had the managers coach them in language. Since I had just finished teaching how to coach, and Svetlana had just finished teaching the ISRs selling skills, this tag team worked very well.

In May, we conducted a Boot Camp for the China dealers using our Mandarin facilitator, Paul Wang. Then in June, Mark and I attended a dealer exchange in Miami for the South American dealers. Although most of the event was in Spanish, we had translators to help us out. Ayus Corcia, a Caterpillar employee, was our facilitator in South and Central America. A native of Spain, Ayus knew Spanish, and as a long-time Caterpillar employee, he understood the product. He attended our domestic Boot Camp, and we certified him to facilitate the program in Spanish.

In July, we kicked off an initiative with Mark Hexum of the marketing division for the Americas to advance the ISR concept into larger machines and product support profiles, called Core. This would involve de-assigning these accounts from the field salespeople and assigning them to telephone sales. After consulting dealers who had implemented the ISR concept, we agreed these representatives should have at least one year of experience serving smaller customers, and the Core ISR position should be a promotion, and perhaps the last step in career development before a field sales position.

In October, Mark and I had the opportunity to travel to Johannesburg, South Africa, to conduct a Boot Camp. The flight we took from Atlanta to Johannesburg was the second-longest flight in the world at that time. We landed in Joberg and were greeted by a driver who would be our right-hand man throughout the trip. At the time of our trip, Nelson Mandela, who led South Africa out of its era of strict segregation and back into the world community, was very ill, and we were worried that if he passed away while we were in country, it would be difficult for us to get around and probably get home.

The training facility in Joberg was fantastic, and had a security system controlled by fingerprints. When they checked us in to security, we found that Mark's fingerprints didn't register sufficiently to work for the system. He thought this was because he is a car buff, and over the years had used quite a bit of sandpaper for delicate work, and he had ground down the ridges on his fingers sufficiently so they didn't register. Throughout the trip, Mark had to follow immediately behind me to get through all the doors we entered and closed as we traversed their campus. Whenever we finished for the day, our driver would be there waiting. In the morning, he would arrive 30 minutes early, and during each drive, he educated us on the unique characteristics of Joberg, including the packed small minivans workers used to get back and forth.

The ISRs we trained and coached had excellent language skills, and we discovered South Africa has many official languages. Almost all the ISRs had second-language capabilities, and customers would flow in and out of English and these second languages. I would be listening to a call in English, and suddenly the customer would switch to Zulu to relate a story, and then switch back to English for technical descriptions of a product support business issue. I also struggled with the names of the ISRs which included "Itumeleng," "Nwabisa" and "Puleng," which the rest of the attendees and managers handled effortlessly.

But I found it hard to call on them without stumbling. But by the end of the Boot Camp, they flowed off my tongue. We left right from the last training session to head home, and Mark and I agreed as we walked out to the car to tip our driver who had been our constant and faithful companion. We cleaned our pockets of all the South African currency we had (Rand) and handed it to the driver. When we related this story to our hosts as we debriefed on the phone when we were home, they told us we had probably given the driver an equivalent of a month's wages, even though it amounted to about $80 for each of us.

While Mark and I were busy with Joberg, Jerome Leonelli, our French facilitator from Paris, conducted a session in France and one in Casablanca, located in a French-speaking area of North Africa. As side projects during 2013, I worked on specific training programs for the oil and gas and marine divisions, and developed a training program for the Core ISR. We also worked on integrating equipment-management solutions into our offerings and training, as well as maintaining a hectic schedule of domestic Boot Camps.

As 2013 ended, the "Journey to a Billion" was 18 months old and right on track.

Chapter 23
CLOSE: Asking for the Sale

"Coffee is for closers!" As Alec Baldwin's character spits out these famous lines from the movie Glengarry Glen Ross, Jack Lemmon, playing the hapless salesperson, turns around in disgust and silently puts the carafe back in the coffee maker. Alex is from downtown, sent on a mission of mercy to teach the pathetic sales group how to close by having the customer sign on the line that is dotted. One quick search in Amazon reveals hundreds of techniques to close, including such old standbys as the "Ben Franklin" close.

When I first got into sales, I bought a small stack of books on closing, and soon recognized that many of them worked well enough. However, in business-to-business relationship selling, I soon realized our goal is not just one sale, but many over time which produce an annuity stream of business. A specific closing technique needed to be used. I settled on what the literature calls the "summary close."

The summary close consists of a trial close to take the buyer's temperature, a business proposal to make sure the salesperson and the customer are on the same page on what the salesperson is asking the customer to buy, and a closing statement. The closing statement is simply a closed-ended question that if the customer says "yes," the sale is done. If the telephone salesperson has built a good relationship with the customer, has explored the business issue at hand, and has navigated the sales cycle effectively, the close should be no big deal. In fact, it should be anticlimactic.

The trial close is a closed-ended question designed to take the buyer's temperature. For example, "Does this make sense to you?" or "Is this what you are looking for?" The goal is to smoke out any objections the customer may have before definitively asking for the sale. Here's an example. Let's say the salesperson just goes right to the close and says, "Can I set up that purchase order for you?" They may get a "no," which is harder to recover from than if they ask first, "How does this sound to you?" With this trial close, the salesperson is likely to hear, something like, "It's okay I guess, but I'm still struggling with your delivery dates." This gives the salesperson more latitude to address than "no." Once a customer has said "no," recovery is far more difficult.

The business proposal has three components — the product or service, the timeline and investment. For example, "I'd recommend you purchase the equipment covered in our proposal with the financing option we discussed. We can have your new equipment ready for delivery in 10 days." Or, "I'd recommend you purchase the two-year term life insurance policy for the low annual investment of $850. With your signature, you are covered."

The close itself is simply a closed-ended question; if answered "yes," it means the telephone salesperson is done. For example, "May I get your new equipment ready for you?" or "May I get your signature?" or "What purchase order number would you like to use?" The summary close is effective over the phone because the salesperson can't see the customer, and may miss some of the important body language clues. By offering a trial close first, to smoke out objections, and then summarizing exactly what they are asking the customer to buy, the summary close avoids any misunderstandings or potential miscues.

These examples have been about closing on a product or service, but the telephone salesperson building relationships over the phone will also close on something else that is critically important — the customer's time. Business-to-business sales often take multiple steps along the sales cycle, and each step along the way, the salesperson is asking the customer to participate in future dialogue.

For example, consider a selling organization which is a laboratory selling testing services for lubricating fluids in industrial machinery. This fluid-testing provides the customer with wear information which helps them schedule preventive maintenance and avoid unscheduled production slowdowns or stoppages. The selling organization has 10,000 accounts, and has nine inside salespeople on the phone who are maintaining 9,000 of those relationships, along with 10 field salespeople who have the largest 1,000 accounts.

The job of the telephone salesperson is to maintain the relationship with the customer, call the customer back to alert them if something is discovered in a sample, and to sell ancillary services which include air monitoring for industrial facilities, both particulate and gasses, waste water sampling and reporting, and industrial exhaust sampling and reporting.

On the first call to a customer, the telephone salesperson will want to close on calling them back if they see something else that can help their business, or if they have an opportunity to save them money on any special or promotion the selling organization may be running. They gain this permission by asking the customer, "If I see something that can help your business, may I give you a call back?" and "If I see an opportunity to save you money on our services, may I give you a call back?"

I've listened to over 13,600 client telephone sales calls and have only heard "no" a few times, and these customers were crabby and we wouldn't want to call them anyway. At the end of the call, the closing process could start out with a business proposal like, "Thank you for your time today. As you requested, I'll give you a call back if I see anything new which may help your business, or if we have a special or promotion which will save you money. In addition, I'll call you if I see any report come through that requires action on your part." The closing process may be completed by asking the closed-ended question, "May I set this up for you?"

Why close on these three things? They don't involve money, but they involve the customer's time. On the next call, the telephone salesperson can open the call with, "You asked me to give you a call back if I saw a report that required action," or "You asked me to give you a call if I saw something new which may help your business," or "You asked me to give you a call if we had a special or promotion which might save you money."

As we discussed under Compelling Reason to Call, this makes the call about the customer, not the inside sales representative. What a great way to position the call! Consider the alternative, "Hi, this is Joe from XYX Testing Lab. I was just calling to touch base, see how things are going." Well Joe, if I were your customer, I'd be irritated you picked up the phone just to "touch base." If I need any bases touched, I'll call you. How about that, Joe?

There are at least four good reasons for closing on the first call for the customer's time. First, it makes the next call about the customer not about the telephone sales representative if done properly. Second, the customer is mentally giving the salesperson the permission to call back, and the customer will allow time for dialogue at the appropriate time.

Third, the customer recognizes that each call will have a business purpose, with a reason for the call and a conclusion at the end of the call. They will appreciate the definition in the relationship, and that talking to this representative has a business purpose. Fourth, a telephone salesperson that closes on each call will find asking for money just another closing statement. Since they close all the time, the money call is just another close. No big deal.

To continue our example, let's assume our telephone salesperson for the testing laboratory calls back on the second call with the purpose of introducing the customer to the selling organization's indoor air testing services. The telephone salesperson walks the customer through the following features/benefits and questions matrix:

Feature	Benefit	Questions to Pre-Qualify
1. Testing validates air quality to federal and state standards	You said compliance with all safety standards is important to you. Our indoor air testing provides validation that federal and state standards are met.	Is compliance with indoor air quality standards important to you?
2. Internet connection allows immediate reporting of violations.	You said immediate notification is critical; our systems are connected to our monitoring facility by the Internet, allowing us to notify you immediately if we observe any problems.	If an air-quality problem occurs, would it be valuable if you could be notified immediately?
3. Air quality impacts employee productivity.	You mentioned productivity is important to your overall business financial health, experts have found air quality directly influences employee productivity.	Is employee productivity important to you and your organization?
4. Air quality is important for some employees who are considering joining an organization.	You told me potential employees may be concerned about the quality of the air in your facility. Our monitoring will allow you to assure them all standards are met.	Have any of your employee applicants raised the issue of indoor air quality when they were considering offers from your firm?

On this second call, the telephone salesperson identifies the first three benefits are important to the customer. The fourth one is not important, because no applicant has ever asked about air quality while applying for a job. When the telephone salesperson did their needs analysis, they also identified the following needs: 1) Our investment in the system needs to be reasonable (price); 2) It must work silently to avoid any noise complaints; and 3) The reports must be easy to understand and interpret. The telephone salesperson closes the customer on the following timeline:

Salesperson: "You indicated improving employee productivity is a strategy you are working on, and the goal is to have results by the end of the year. Because of this, you indicated if you decided to move forward, you'd want the system installed by September 1st. Is that correct?"

Customer: "Yes. We'd want to see documentation by year end."

Salesperson: "Good. If you were to move forward with our offering, we'd need about a month to get everything set up and online. Do you think you'll be in a position to make a decision about this system by August 1st?"

Customer: "We'd be able to do that, sure."

Salesperson: "Great. I'd suggest that between now and then we go through these steps. First, we'll set up a time to review the standard reports to make sure they meet your interpretation and easy-to-understand needs. On this same call, I'd suggest we review the air-quality standards so you can see how the report supports compliance, and review some independent studies of how air quality impacts productivity. If everything meets with your approval on this call, I'll set up a conference call with you, me, and one of our reporting analysts so you can be comfortable with our alert system. Finally, I'll put together a quotation on your needs, and review it with you over the phone by July 20th, to give you plenty of time before a decision needs to be made. Does this sound like a good plan to you?" <trial close>

Customer: "Sounds like a good plan to me."

Salesperson: "Great. We'll follow the plan we just established. Our first call should take about 30 minutes or so. <business proposal> Does 10:00 next Tuesday work for you for our first call?" <closing statement>

By closing on the timeline, the salesperson can make each step in the sales process about the customer, not about them. For example, on the next call at 10:00 next Tuesday, the telephone salesperson can open the call, "You asked me to give you a call today to review ..." At the end of this call, the salesperson should close on the next step in the sales process they defined on the first call.

Salesperson: "The next step we agreed upon was for us to set up a time to talk to one of our internal experts. This call should take about 30 minutes, as well. <business proposal> Does 11:00 next Monday work for you?" <closing statement>

The business proposal is the product or service, timeline, and investment. In this case, the investment is simply the 30-minute time commitment, the product or service is the consultation with the internal expert, and

11:00 next Monday is the timeline.

On the final call, when the proposal is reviewed, the telephone salesperson should ask a trial close, and then, if no objections surface, ask for the sale, even though it is 10 days ahead of the decision date. If the customer is ready to go, it's time to be done. If the customer asks for more time, the telephone salesperson can always call back.

Salesperson: "How does our proposal look to you?" *<trial close>*

Customer: "Looks pretty good."

Salesperson: "Then I'd suggest you install the air monitoring system in our proposal and begin increasing productivity and meeting air-quality standards, 24 hours a day, seven days a week. May we get the system in place for you?"

Closing on every call sets up the next call to make it about the customer. Closing on the timeline creates a defined sales cycle driving toward a customer deadline, avoiding a stall and providing a pathway for the telephone salesperson. Asking for the sale closes the business.

Celebrate the close. Coffee is for closers. And perhaps after hours, when the sale is closed, champagne is in order, too!

Chapter 24
Across the Table

In 2014, the telephone sales program joined the "Across the Table" initiative, which Caterpillar launched globally. The book "Across the Table" had been written in 1926 and described the relationship between Caterpillar and its dealer network. The relationship had been fostered and developed over the years based on trust and performance. One of the deliverables was to look at coverage, and to help each dealer maximize their touch points with customers, and to assure the appropriate level of coverage was assigned — marketing, telephone sales, or field sales.

By this time, we had developed implementation guidebooks and training for a variety of target markets, including machine sales, product support, and power systems, as well as marine. Beginning in 2013, we began to study how to sell larger machines and how to cover larger customers using telephone sales. The "Across the Table" consultants and internal experts began wrestling with their coverage models and what was the best metrics to provide the best customer satisfaction.

We'd had customers who were the biggest and most important accounts in a telephone sales territory become the smallest, least important accounts in a field sales territory when they were transferred, because of growth. It almost seemed like the customer was penalized for buying more. The telephone sales representative would call once or twice a month, the field sales representative could only afford to stop by once or twice a year.

The "Across the Table" teams worked with us to determine what the best way of covering each type of customer was, and transition paths as a customer grew or a customer's business changed. Mark was involved in dozens of meeting at various locations, wrestling with numbers, sketching models, making notes on PowerPoint slides. Finally, a consensus was reached, and the team began making the rounds to each dealer.

For us, this represented the first time the telephone sales program had become part of a big internal initiative rather than an organic, primarily dealer-driven program. Mark had been the primary steward of the program internally, navigating the corporate landmines, along with support management. But to his credit, he kept the focus on the dealers.

Now, after nine years, the telephone sales platform was part of a global initiative.

In retrospect, I think Mark was unusually wise politically, keeping the focus on the dealer and the customer. It was frustrating to me as an outsider at times, understanding the necessity of running the political trap lines to avoid the appearance that this was "cooked up in the Caterpillar kitchen." But, my staff often remarked that salespeople and dealers would share information with us they would be reluctant to share if this was seen to be a corporate initiative.

Mark often talked about programs that were "dealer insurance." In other words, the dealer reluctantly embraced a corporate initiative, because they wanted to keep their dealership, as opposed to "dealer pull." With "dealer pull" the dealer implemented the concept because it's a good idea for their dealership and customers. Mark had succeeded in guiding the telephone selling ISR initiative along through "dealer pull." By 2015, the socialization, developmental and experimentation phases were past and the entire focus was on implementation and spreading best practices. By the end of 2015, we were within an eyelash of a billion dollars, with over 650 telephone sales representatives in place globally — two years early.

Bill Buss retired from teaching our Boot Camps in early 2015, although we pull him out of retirement to help. Mark Wankel retired at the end of 2015 and joined Business Performance Group as a senior consultant, helping clients who have similar challenges. Hundreds of telephone sales representatives have moved on to senior positions at dealerships. Many who attended the first Boot Camps are now managers, and are sending their telephone salespeople. Others have moved into management. Many have moved into field sales.

On our frequent business trips, Mark and I often talk about our lessons learned. The first lesson we agree is the establishment of a defensible and clear business model, to convince owners to pony up the money to invest in telephone sales. Second, the benefit of using our "iron triangle" of socialization — dealer exchanges, where dealers talk to dealers, implementation guidebooks, where managers and implementers can find the resources they need to deploy, and training — both for managers and telephone salespeople. We also supplemented training by creating quarterly newsletters and monthly telephone conferences to build a community and encourage interaction.

We placed an emphasis on finding the right person, and on focusing on salesperson selection. Early on, we learned how important this was, and it became a recurring theme. Mark kicked off each dealer exchange by stating clearly, "If you aren't doing what you need to do to hire the right person, stop." I took this advice to heart.

Finally, and I give Mark all the credit for this, he astutely weaved his way through the corporate and OEM/dealer politics successfully for a decade. He avoided the "flavor of the month" problem by refusing to undermine his well-thought-out campaign to keep the ISR program a dealer initiative with corporate support, not the other way around. He supported other initiatives by leveraging inside sales to sell their products and services, listened to dealers intently, and traveled exhaustively to be an advocate.

He educated a multitude of managers and leaders, showing immense patience and versatility. Many times, during the journey, we discussed a corporate meeting he was summoned to attend, and I remarked he had such patience to be explaining again how the telephone selling program worked, what it did and the results it had accomplished. He would tell me of a roadblock he was working on, and it seemed insurmountable to me at the time. And then, a few weeks later without much fanfare, the roadblock would become just more pavement under his feet. And on we moved.

That's how you complete a journey to a billion.

Chapter 25
Selling Business Services in a Product World

The title of this chapter refers to a basic difficulty in selling services. Services are intangible while products are tangible. Think of how this intangibility influences how we even refer to services by grabbing nomenclature from something physical. We say we will "fly" rather than "using an air transport provider." We "go to a hospital" rather than "receiving health services." And we "go to school" rather than "participate in educational opportunities." With services accounting for almost 80% of the U.S. economy, many business-to-business sellers offer services, whether they are offered as a cross-sell with a product, or as a stand-alone service business. Many telephone salespeople find themselves selling services either in conjunction with products, or as a unique offering.

Products are manufactured and produced under controlled conditions, which reduces variability. For years, manufacturers have worked to stamp out variability and produce products within tightly managed specifications. Services require the interaction of customers and employees of the service provider, making it difficult to standardize and control variability. For services, the ability to adjust, tailor, and customize to the customer is often celebrated. Two worlds.

Services offer a unique challenge to the salesperson. Services have heterogeneity, which means the output cannot be standardized, and the involvement of each unique customer changes the output. This requires the salesperson to educate the customer and in turn educate the organization about the customer's unique requirements. Anyone who has ever played a game of telephone, passing along a message from one person to another until it turns into a garbled mess understands the complexity of this.

Unlike products, service cannot be inventoried and pulled off the shelf. There is no such thing as an inventory of services as they are uniquely perishable. If your business is selling repair services for example, and no one needs a technician on Friday, that time cannot be inventoried until Monday. Therefore, the organization must be able to meet demand as the salesperson sells it, creating tension between the selling organization and those that deliver the service.

The issue of heterogeneity, or non-standardized outputs, causes some organizations to work around these communication difficulties by using the "propose and deliver" sales model, most commonly found in consulting organizations. With this model, the salesperson sells the engagement and then goes out and delivers the service. The advantage is there are few communication issues between salesperson and service delivery person, since they are the same individual. The disadvantage for the selling organization is growth is very difficult.

Because the consultant owns the entire customer experience from engagement through delivery, they have little loyalty toward the selling organization. At some point, the consultant/salesperson may feel the cut of the action going to their company is wasted. After all, they are doing all the work. "Propose and deliver" sales organizations may fly apart due to centrifugal force, as their salespeople/consultants are drawn into their customer's orbits.

Organizations that want the customer experience shared between a salesperson and service delivery group are generally more stable, and more able to grow. The drawback is the need for the salesperson to communicate the service delivery requirements internally. This often leads to computer screens requesting data, meetings called to discuss clients, documentation, and a sales manager who is able and willing to play referee.

A drawback, too, is the natural tendency to narrow the range of service offerings to fit the 20% of the opportunities that result in 80% of the business—The Pareto Principle of service delivery. So, into this mix comes the telephone salesperson. The salesperson is charged with selling a service, which is at its nature intangible. It can't be felt, tasted, seen, or heard easily, with huge communication requirements on the back end. To top it off, customers, in all their variety and with differing needs and expectations, must be satisfied.

Customers also evaluate services differently. A few years ago, a relative of mine went in for heart surgery to have a pacemaker installed. I asked her about the experience when she returned home, and she told me the nurses were great but the food wasn't very good. As we talked, I smiled to myself thinking, "You just experienced a service which probably saved your life, and you evaluated the food and the nurses." When she purchased this pacemaker installation, she did little research about the skills of the surgeon (he was board certified — a verification attribute), none about the brand of pacemaker used. I don't think she was aware there is more than one. She trusted the surgeon.

The experience was evaluated in the rearview mirror by what she could get her mental arms around — the nurses and the food. All of us would probably walk on coals to get a pacemaker if that was required to solve a heart issue. The hospital, the device manufacture, the surgeon, and the surgical team encompass a huge investment in executing the surgery flawlessly and safely, and the post-procedure evaluation all comes down to soggy French fries prepared by a short order cook and delivered by an entry-level orderly. The chaotic life of a service provider.

In my business, I've slaved over a training course, researching each page, field testing each concept, educating and evaluating the presenter, only to have a participant complain and ding us because we got a small smudge on their certificate of completion, acquired somewhere in the mail. Sell the dream. Service the nightmare.

The Sales Manager in Service Sales

A sales manager for a selling organization selling services or a product organization that is adding or expanding a service offering must consider carefully how these services are positioned in the marketplace. Many services are experiential. They need to be experienced to be evaluated and enjoyed, and therefore careful positioning is extremely valuable to provide a mental signpost for the customer, and to put definition and structure around something that might otherwise seem vague and fuzzy. For example, many product producers sell as a service "extended warranties" and "customer support agreements." In the former, the selling organization will extend the warranty coverage of the product into the future for a fee, and in the latter, the selling organization will perform a prescribed set of maintenance offerings into the future.

Many organizations offer these services as cross-sell items once a customer has purchased the product. "Oh by the way, would you like either an extended warranty or customer support agreement where we'll do your routine maintenance for a while?" The difficulty of positioning this becomes apparent when you consider the discussion in this book about how business-to-business companies evaluate risk. The customer has just gone through the time period when they are most worried about risk — just before the sale closes.

They have overcome their fears and agreed to buy, and the salesperson infers they just made a risky purchase by indicating extending the warranty is a good idea. Wouldn't they like to buy an insurance policy called an extended warranty, and wouldn't they like to purchase something to take care of all that pesky maintenance they just signed up for? Whew!

In many product purchases, the salesperson deals with price objections.

Some negotiation takes place perhaps, then a price is agreed upon. The buyer mentally accepts the cost of the product, and immediately after they say "yes," the salesperson attempts to raise the price with extended warranties — maybe a customer support agreement. And the customer, who now has their investment firmly in their brain, finds it difficult to reopen the mental negotiations — even if the extended warranty, customer support agreement, and perhaps other services make business sense. Because of these challenges, customer acceptance of ancillary services may be suboptimal.

In many instances, the sales manager may need to study their market, and test positioning services into the sale early, so services can be closed, along with the product. For example, if the selling organization is selling an elevator for a high-rise building, they may add steps to the sales cycle to evaluate whether an extended warranty and preventive maintenance agreement would be valuable for the buyer to consider.

This has three major benefits for the telephone salesperson. First, because the services are part of the sales cycle, the salesperson can involve the remainder of the buying committee and do all the additional needs analysis and presentations that may be required. Second, by their nature, many services reduce the inherent risk of purchasing the product. An extended warranty means the customer does not have to worry about a premature failure much further into the future. A customer support agreement means the customer doesn't need to worry about figuring out how to maintain what they are considering purchasing. Other services may also serve to reduce the customer's perception of risk. Third, when the final proposal is on the table, the salesperson's offering is likely to be an apple to the competitor's orange. The extra services make side-by-side comparisons difficult, making customer decisions strictly on price seem risky.

Sometimes managers decide the best positioning is to offer an entry service or product at a low price, and then use the relationship to sell additional services after the initial purchase, not as a cross-sell but as a new sales cycle. For example, a payroll service may sell the basic payroll processing at a low entry price, and then leverage the relationship and their knowledge of the customer's payroll to sell workman's compensation or liability insurance, online training, or anything else tied to a knowledge of payroll. In this case, they may position themselves as competing on value originally — payroll processing at a low price — and they may re-position themselves as a human resource consultant once the original sale is completed.

What if the selling organization just positioned themselves as a human resource consultant right off the bat, offered a buffet of services to help businesses manage benefits, payroll, training, and insurances? For some customers, this may be more attractive. For others, less. It may also make it far more difficult to close the original sale, and to turn a prospect into a customer. A good vertical positioning strategy along with the horizontal positioning of entry into the buying process is needed.

Sales managers must help their salespeople construct bulletproof sales cycles. Services, by their nature, often have some features that can be independently verified, some features that must be experienced to be understood, and other features where the buying organization must trust the selling organization. For example, a selling organization of Certified Public Accountants can proudly display their CPA certificates on the wall, on their website and promotional materials.

Their skills at being accountants has been verified by a certifying body. Prospective customers can verify this for themselves by observing the seal of approval. For experience features, the selling organization may invite a potential buyer into their "service factory" to meet their people and experience some of what they would purchase. Or, the selling organization may give away some small element of the service so the buyer can participate in an experience before committing — like a free trial. In other cases, the buyer must simply trust the seller.

If the telephone salesperson uncovers a need that could be addressed by an experience feature, they need to add an experience step into the sales cycle if possible. If they find a need covered by a verification feature, they need to provide the support which verifies the feature is held, such as an independent party verification (badging). If they find a trust feature, they need to build the relationship sufficiently so trust is established, and consider case studies, referrals and the like.

The sales manager must study the features of their service and determine which features are verifiable, which are experience, and which are trust. Once this exercise is complete, they must determine how the salespeople will support each of these. For example, consider a selling organization delivering a service of property maintenance for owner-occupied commercial buildings. Among the features and benefits they have are the following:

Feature	Benefit
TRUST: If a security alert occurs after business hours, we will respond with the police to secure your property.	You said you want peace of mind, our security services will respond during nonbusiness hours to work with the authorities to protect your property.
EXPERIENCE: We take care of all external grounds maintenance, including snow removal, mowing, tree trimming, and ornamental flower and shrubbery maintenance.	You said you want beautiful and well-maintained grounds. Our crews will take care of everything outside – including snow removal and assuring your grounds are completely well maintained and attractive.
VERIFIABLE: All our employees undergo random drug tests, and we thoroughly screen all applicants before hiring.	You said you want assurances that all contract employees on your premises are fully qualified. All our employees undergo random drug tests and go through a battery of extensive screening before they are ever on our payroll.
EXPERIENCE: We will monitor your grounds 24 X 7, 365 days a year by video surveillance system.	You said you want peace of mind, and to know during holidays, evenings and weekends, your property is protected. Our video surveillance system will be on duty 24 x 7, 365 days a year.

If the telephone salesperson qualifies the first feature for a prospective customer, "If a security alert occurs after business hours, we will respond with the police to secure your property," it would be evaluated by trust. This is because, until the customer signs a contract, and until the customer has an event like this, they will just have to trust the selling organization will perform. How could the sales manager support this trust feature for the salespeople? Testimonials from current customers, perhaps copies of police reports showing they were onsite, or case studies of how they responded and the result are all good examples.

If the telephone salesperson qualifies the second feature for a prospective customer, "We take care of all external grounds maintenance, including snow removal, mowing, tree trimming and ornamental flower and shrubbery maintenance," how could the sales manager support this feature? They could offer tours of various customer sites showing the maintenance of the grounds (or snow removal in winter), they could take videos of their crews in action and post them online. Or if a prospective customer comes onsite to the "service factory," they can have a crew foreman meet with the customer to discuss how they would service their property.

Finally, if the telephone salesperson identifies "all our employees undergo random drug tests, and we thoroughly screen all applicants before hiring" as a critical feature, it can be verified by a third party. For example, a drug-testing company's certification that they randomly test their employees and a screening bureau's certification on the background checking they perform could be made available by the sales manager for the salespeople to distribute. After all privacy, anonymity and confidentiality requirements are met, of course.

Telephone Salespeople in Service Sales

The telephone salesperson in a non-propose and deliver model has a special set of challenges. They are selling something intangible that has heterogeneity. Where strict uniformity is celebrated with products, the ability to customize, adapt, and differentiate is praised with services. These salesperson challenges include teaching customers their roles, dealing with diverse buying committees, figuring out who might turn into a bad customer, documenting carefully, and dealing with price comparisons.

Because customers often participate in the consumption of a service, they must be taught their roles. Several years ago, I was flying out of a nearby city, and as I pulled into the long-term parking lot there was a big line in front of the areas where you'd normally get a ticket and enter. I was puzzled, because usually this is a quick procedure. When it was my turn, I saw the terminal no longer gave out tickets. The driver was expected to swipe a credit card and then park. When the driver left the parking lot after their trip, they would use the same credit card to leave the ramp which would be charged the appropriate amount. This all took place without the traditional ticket. A large sign was posted near the gate explaining the charges, but it was hard to read at 6 a.m. and customers were frustrated because they were expecting a ticket.

As I left the garage, I rode in an elevator full of angry customers. One said his wife was coming to pick up their car, and she had different credit cards than he did. How was she going to get out of the lot, he asked? Another said because of the long line waiting to get in, she was afraid of missing her flight. A third said this was his second time under the new system, and it seemed to work well. But he was tired of waiting in line while everyone else figured it out.

Even with a simple service like a parking ramp, customers need to be taught their roles. What do they need to do to consume the service successfully and with maximum customer satisfaction? If your company does tax preparation services, what information does the customer need to gather for you to prepare the returns? If you offer HVAC maintenance services for commercial buildings, how do you gain access to the systems? How are you electronically notified of any problems, and how does this software tie into your systems? Often salespeople need to educate customers just to provide them with a quotation. This requires a great deal of patience, understanding, and training.

Next, telephone salespeople must realize that when selling a service, different members of the buying committee may request unique customizations and may have specialized viewpoints of the service. Customer needs and risks must be carefully captured and defined from the entire buying committee, and the differences must be managed.

Salespeople may recognize incompatibilities among the buying committee needs, and may need to reconcile these differences before advancing the sales process. The sales cycle itself is often more complex, because a significant amount of trust must be established. Because services may involve extensive interactions between the staffs of the selling and buying organizations, cultural differences and ways of doing business may need to be recognized, understood, and communicated, and appropriate adjustments put into place.

The salesperson must also figure out who may be a bad customer — a customer who asks the organization to do something they don't do well. In the product world where items are manufactured in controlled conditions away from the customer, the organization is indifferent in many ways to variability among customers.

When a product organization calls someone a "bad customer," they are typically a bad credit-risk or someone who will use the product in ways for which it is not intended — possibly causing harm to themselves or others. In the service world where customers are participants in the service process, the organization is extremely sensitive to variability among customers. In the service world, a "bad customer" is not limited to one who is a bad credit risk. A "bad customer" is also one who demands service aspects outside of what is normally delivered.

The salesperson must also document carefully. As mentioned elsewhere in this book, this is already a staple in the life of the telephone salesperson, who usually juggles 600 to 800 accounts and possibly more. If the salesperson is selling services however, they usually have documentation requirements beyond simple order entry or maintaining a customer narrative and demographic information. They may need to document specific interaction instructions, and document what level of training has been conducted during the sales process to assure the handoff to the selling organization is conducted seamlessly.

Finally, with many services, price comparisons may be difficult. Because of the variability of services, it is hard not for the selling organization's service to be an apple to a competitor's orange. The benefit to the telephone salesperson is services tend to be less price-competitive, because direct comparisons are difficult to make. It also places a premium on negotiation skills, because when the telephone salesperson's organization is the preferred supplier, and the buyer can't base their price discovery on direct comparisons to competitor's quotations, they may feel obligated to negotiate due to the lack of price discovery alternatives.

The Keys to Selling Services Over the Phone

Because of the challenges of managing a service-selling telephone organization, and in being a salesperson selling service, there is a wide range of outcomes between different selling organizations. To be successful, marketing, and sales must work closely together. In many industries, the sales cycle for new customers into a service organization is long.

For example, if the selling organization is offering building cleaning services to property owners, they may need to wait for existing contracts to expire or other business drivers which will prompt the potential customer to consider switching. Marketing should work with sales to determine trigger emails and other marketing automation assistance to keep customers warm in between phone calls. Marketing will also need to help create sales collateral — electronic, online, and printed — which support verification and trust features which may be identified by potential customers as important to them.

The selling organization's service providers will probably also need to be part of the sales mix. In the example above of cleaning services, a potential customer may want to visit a building where the selling organization's service employees are cleaning, engaging these employees in the sales process. If the selling organization is selling medical services, a potential customer may talk to a nurse or an intake specialist, involving them in the selling process.

The selling organization should consider creating a blueprint of their service delivery and support operations, and identify all areas where customers interface with the organization, and what are "back office functions," out of sight of the customer.

The sales manager along with marketing, can then create a features/benefits matrix, and determine where the need for experiences in the selling cycle may require service delivery personnel to interact with potential customers. The telephone salespeople should be fully trained on these experiences, and should shadow delivery personnel to be totally comfortable with the process.

Unfortunately, it is easy to try to sell services without preparation and forethought. Many telephone salespeople have been handed a directory of suspects, a telephone and a rudimentary contact management system and have been told to go forward and "make it happen."

What usually happens in this scenario instead is a frustrated salesperson and low sales. In my experience, I have seen a wider variance of success among service sellers than product sellers, and I've found that most product sellers struggle to sell ancillary services because they adopt a product mindset.

It is a product world; it is easier to grasp the tangible, and buyers are on firmer ground when considering physical objects with similar characteristics shipped almost anywhere. But there's money to be made in selling services over the phone. It's worth the time and energy to get it right.

Chapter 26
CHECK: Assuring Customer Satisfaction

In the early years of Business Performance Group, we had a client who, among other things, made components for spacesuits used by NASA in the space shuttle program. After the first presentation we delivered, I called the manager of the initiative we were supporting to see how it went. She exclaimed, "It was great. He didn't die!" I was taken aback. I was happy our instructor didn't die during the session, but it seemed like a strange first comment. I pressed a little further, thinking "die" perhaps meant the show business term for a bad performance.

She continued, "The last time we had an out-of-town presenter, he died in the hotel room before the event and it was traumatic on everyone. It's been hard for us to get over it. So, we're happy your guy showed up healthy and ready to go." Okay, this remains the most interesting CHECK call I've ever had. It turned out the session went very well, and he didn't die — in both uses of the term. CHECK is to complete the post-purchase evaluation buyers make, where they judge whether they made a good decision buying from the selling organization.

The final step in our telephone sales model is to CHECK back with the customer to assure what they purchased met their expectation. This is a special challenge with services, because customers may evaluate the selling organization based on tangential factors, such as the quality of food during a hospital stay, and not the quality of medical care. In a product sale, evaluations tend to be more straightforward. Checking back with the customer is an easy, compelling reason to call, it builds and strengthens the relationship, and it sets up the next sale.

For the telephone sales representative calling business-to-business, the customer service call, the CHECK in our model, is the easiest, compelling reason to call. Customer service is intuitively supportive, and it makes an easy opening to the next call. "Tammy, last month you purchased an induction fan for your primary evacuation pump motor. Did our product and our customer service meet your expectations?" The telephone representative should have sales and relationship building reasons for the call, as well. But this compelling reason to call is a great call opening. Of course, if there are any lingering issues of customer dissatisfaction with the order, these need to be out on the table before the representative can ask for more business or build the relationship anyway.

A customer has both needs and expectations that arise from any encounter with a member of the selling organization. Customer needs are usually tangible, and early in this course I presented how a telephone sales representative could probe for those needs. Customer expectations are often intangible. Expectations center on how any contact with the selling organization is managed and handled, and how any issues raised during the contact are addressed. Expectations of the customer include being treated with respect, treated professionally, listened to, cared for, appreciated, and gratitude expressed for their business.

Needs first. The telephone salesperson should have embedded in their customer narrative the needs the customer articulated during the sales process. They should CHECK with the customer that these needs were met. If the telephone salesperson knows their product or service well, they should be comfortable their product met these needs. Therefore, this quick review with the customer will reinforce their satisfaction with what they received, and catch any problems. The last step of the buying process is to review how the product or service met the buyer's needs.

Next expectations. Beyond the product or service the customer purchased, they also evaluate how the process of procurement occurred, and any interaction they had with the selling organization during the procurement process. Earlier, you learned the telephone sales representative should probe for customer expectations during their discussion of buying committee, so any expectations the customer articulated should also be in their notes. Besides what customers articulate directly, expectations included being "treated with respect," "treated professionally," and "listened to."

The telephone sales representative should ask questions about the procurement process, to make sure all these expectations were met. The telephone sales representative has invested a great deal of energy and time building the relationship with the customer. This can be dissipated in a heartbeat by a careless customer service agent, an indifferent delivery driver, a non-communicative installer or by overly aggressive accounting personnel. The better the relationship the telephone sales representative has with the customer, the higher the customer's expectations will be during the procurement process.

Sales managers are responsible for mediating between the telephone sales group and the rest of the selling organization. The better the relationships the salespeople develop, the higher procurement expectations will rise, and the more the sales manager will find him or herself working with the rest of the selling organization to improve their processes. This process of managing the customer experience is complex, because it doesn't involve the selling organization's product or service. It is more a matter of how customers take ownership of it and how customer interactions are managed.

Expectations of the customer also include being appreciated, and gratitude expressed for their business. When the telephone salesperson CHECKs on an order, they must express appreciation again for the order and tell the customer how grateful they are they chose to do business with their firm. It seems like every time I take a flight, a flight attendant or pilot says, "I know you have a choice when you fly. Thank you for flying with us." The telephone salesperson must close this loop with the customer.

Checking back after the sale also builds the relationship. Small problems can be resolved, big issues can be aired, and how the telephone sales representative handles each of these reinforces the trust the customer has in the selling organization. If the selling organization's customers produce an annuity stream of business, not one-off sales, the customer service provided during the CHECK phase can increase the customer's perceived switching cost to a new provider. For example, the customer may think, "Every vendor has problems occasionally. At least I know if I have a problem with XYZ, my sales representative will handle it." This is a hard hill for a competitor to climb.

Finally, CHECK sets up the next sale. If there are any lingering issues, CHECKing will lead to discovery, which will lead to resolution. Expressing gratitude and appreciation will check a mental box with the customer and lead to what comes next. If the telephone sales representative has opened the call with the customer service compelling reason to call, and needs were met and expectations exceeded, it's time to move to build the relationship and uncover additional needs.

The telephone sales representative can heave a big sigh and move on; the selling organization didn't die on the last sale, in either sense of the term.

Chapter 27
I Like Your Style!

Years ago, a client was very frustrated because her inbound customer service team didn't meet its cross-selling and up-selling objectives. The mission was clear. If the customer ordered "Y," offer them "X" and "Z," both of which complemented the product they were purchasing. For every product in their catalog, there were a few ancillary products or services to offer.

Up-selling wasn't any more complicated. For each product in the catalog, there was a service component that included the product and statement, "We can do it for you!" The key to cross- and up-selling was to ask a good transition question, "Would you like a way to…" position the benefits, and ask for the sale. If the customer said no, you thank them and process the original order.

I put on a headset and listened to some calls. On some calls, the representatives did just as they had been instructed. As they entered a certain product, their order entry screens would show the related cross- and up-selling items. They'd go through the process, and about one out of five times, they'd get the additional order. However, I noted that about 50% of the time they didn't ask. They just took the original order, thanked the customer, and ended the call. Why?

They said they could just tell the customer wasn't interested. There was something in the tone of the customer's voice, the fact that they were to the point, which expressed they wouldn't be interested. Other customers seemed like they had already done all the research that was necessary. If they wanted more products than their original order, they would have placed the additional orders. I noticed that customers who were pleasant on the phone, and engaged in a little banter with the inbound representative always were asked about the cross- and up-sell items, in a pleasant way, of course.

I proposed to my client that we have two team meetings (we needed to keep at least half the team on the phone and needed to meet at the end of the day). During the meetings, I'd administer the instrument, "What's My Selling Style?" from HRDQ (HRDQ.com) and we'd go through the exercises contained within. This instrument, based on the work by Marston which underlies many of the popular personality assessments including DISC, reveals the dominant selling style of the participant, in this case, the inbound customer service team.

The four quadrants are "Systematic," "Direct," "Spirited," and "Considerate." "Considerate" people struggle most with people who are "direct" — their opposite style. They also struggle to a lesser extent with those who are "systematic" and "spirited" and of course prosper with those who are also "considerate."

I found almost all the inbound team was considerate. This isn't a surprise; after all, the name of the team is "customer service." The title alone would lead one to believe "considerate" people would be attracted to this position. As we went through the exercises, I explained that "direct" customers, and to a lesser extent "systematic" and "spirited," simply had a different style. For direct, just tell them what you'd recommend they do. For those who are systematic, explain how purchasing the cross- or up-sell item was a logical step. For spirited, try to capture, bottle, and bounce back some of their boundless enthusiasm by explaining how their experience can be maximized by buying these additional items! We then went through the section of the instrument that indicates how to identify a customer's style over the phone.

We got an 18% increase in cross- and up-selling and did nothing else.

This reinforced my belief that communication style awareness is critical for salespeople, and especially critical for the telephone salesperson selling business-to-business. As we've discussed in this book before, the fact that the salesperson and customer usually have only one ear engaged (unless either party is using a dual headset), and due to the lack of body language, it is easy to misconstrue a situation.

In our cross- and up-selling course for telephone salespeople, we use four different video segments showing in turn, a "direct," "considerate," "spirited" and "systematic" person engaging a salesperson with the identical transaction. All that is different is the style of the customer. It is eye opening to recognize how style influences how the transaction is perceived, even though the facts of the situation don't change.

Style influences the customer/salesperson relationship throughout. The telephone salesperson and customer relationship typically goes through four stages: 1) First call, 2) Initial transaction(s), 3) Relationship and market share growth, 4) Annuity stream and maintenance. During the first call, the salesperson is trying to convince the potential buyer it's worth his or her time to explore doing business. The telephone salesperson must come across as goal oriented. There must be some economic reason for pursuing a relationship or nothing will happen. The salesperson must uncover this economic reason.

Within this goal orientation, if the customer is direct, the salesperson must be to the point. If the customer is spirited, the salesperson must generate considerable enthusiasm. If the customer is considerate, the salesperson must show concern for them as a buyer, and if the buyer is systematic, heaven help the salesperson. (I'm systematic.) No, if the buyer is systematic, the salesperson must explore a series of logical steps to see if they should be doing business together.

The salesperson should mirror the communication style of the buyer as much as possible. During the first call, it is unlikely the buyer will put any verbal distance between him or herself and the organization. For example, they may use language like "all of our vendors must comply with regulation 14-7 of the Northwest Regional Commercial Code."

During the initial transaction phase, the telephone salesperson is trying to convince the buyer his or her offering is the best available, and the selling organization is a trustworthy partner. The telephone salesperson must demonstrate they are highly interested in this relationship. By this point, they may have communicated on the phone several times, it is likely the buyer will begin to share some personal information.

The seller must be aware of the buyer's communication style, and adjust accordingly, although some of the salesperson's natural style will begin to come through. It is also likely the buyer may begin to put just a little distance between themselves and the organization. The salesperson may begin to hear, "Well, around here they like what your competitor does regarding payment terms."

During market share and relationship growth phase, this goes one of two directions — either the buyer and telephone salesperson build a personal bond that allows them to banter about the weather, sports, and local events, or the conversation tends to remain focused on business. If a personal bond is established, the sales representative tends to gently glide back into their natural style, and if you listen to these conversations, you can tell successful representatives continue to adjust to the style of the buyer. But the personality you know when they are off the phone is very apparent.

If the conversations tend to remain focused on all business, the successful representative remains style conscious, and you can detect, as you listen to these phone calls, a difference between the person you know and the voice you are hearing. Customers and representatives who establish a personal bond will both tend to distance themselves conversationally a little more from their businesses.

A customer may talk of political challenges within their organization, and provide guidance to the representative on how to maneuver through the thicket of purchasing regulations.

When the annuity stream and maintenance phase is reached, the telephone representative may have multiple contacts within the buying organization. With their primary buyer, they should have easy-flowing conversations, which start out on a personal level and then transition to business. They should know the likes and dislikes of their buyer, should adjust their styles as more of a learned response on how to deal with this person, rather than just guidance from an instrument like "What's My Selling Style?" That's because they have a considerable track record and conversational history with this person. With secondary contacts, the conversations may be less personal, and style guidance more necessary.

Not all relationships flow like this, of course. I have several clients I obtained when I first started Business Performance Group that I fully adjust my style to communicate with them. And they put little distance between themselves and the organization, although they are good clients with years of mutual history. The reality is, if you were to work my client base, you'd get deeper personally in some relationships and shallower in others than I have. It's because we are different. We will click with different people and different personalities. The same is true of any personalities out there who pick up a phone.

When I was a sales manager, I had a telephone salesperson who was working for me who was an ex-Marine. He was the hardest worker in the department. My quota was 60 dials per day and he did 100 routinely. As I listened to his calls, I could tell that he was trying hard to match the styles of each of his buyers. Though he wasn't as easygoing as many of the representatives, he was relentless in finding out the needs of his buyers, adapting to situations and picking up the phone.

He rarely had the lengthy, personal relationship calls that others did, but he was respected because of his work ethic, and tireless devotion to his customers' needs. He was always one of our top producers. What I learned is successful salespeople learn to adjust to the styles of the buyers, and that the longer they talk to someone on multiple calls, the more they learn how to best communicate with each buyer.

What's your selling style?

Chapter 28
Omnichannel Marketing — Personal Telephone Selling in the Connected Age

An original equipment manufacturer of forklifts has an established dealer in Anytown. The Anytown Dealership has a customer with a warehouse located in a new industrial area of town. The warehouse is highly automated with most of the warehouse dark at times (robotic pickers do not need light), and their forklifts are used to position pallets and other bulky materials in an endless ballet from truck and rail car to shelf to customer.

Each of the forklifts owned by the warehouse and sold by the Anytown Dealer are connected to the Internet. Every operating hour, which is basically 24 hours a day except for a few major holidays, each forklift uploads information on performance and data points regarding preventive maintenance opportunities. When fluids are changed, they are also sent in for analysis to determine if there is unusual contamination or wear particles that might indicate a future problem. Special sensors on components detect changes in vibration and temperature patterns that might indicate future problems. Everything is fine-tuned to prevent an unscheduled breakdown.

A telephone salesperson is assigned to the account by the Anytown Dealer, and she juggles about 500 accounts, calling the typical customer four times a year. The dealer's information system monitors each of the 2,120 pieces of equipment in her territory, and alerts her to opportunities to perform preventive maintenance to keep the equipment running. She also receives the fluid analysis reports and any recommendations from the dealer's condition monitoring department that impact her customers. If a trend is identified, she calls the customer and discusses possible solutions.

Some of her customers own their equipment outright and do most of their maintenance with advice from the dealer. In this case, she sells parts and maintenance supplies. Others do some of the work but rely on the dealership to do the more complicated repairs. The customer changes oil, the dealership changes components. Others have entered into a customer support agreement with the dealership and the dealership handles all maintenance. In many cases, the customer does not own the equipment, the dealership does, and the customer pays by hours of usage.

The dealership offers online forklift safety and operations training for new operators. Some customers pay by usage. Others have these services bundled with their agreements. The telephone salesperson sells these services, as well. The dealership offers an inspection app, usable on almost any smartphone, which allows the operators to perform a visual inspection on each shift. This information is uploaded and stored as part of each machine's online history and is used for preventive maintenance. Sometimes this service is sold by the telephone sales rep. Other times it's included in a customer support agreement.

Customers can find all the specifications of any forklift online. These include the performance of various fuel options (diesel, electric, and natural gas), lifting capabilities, turning ratios, etc. The dealership sends customized trigger marketing emails out to customers based on options selected by the telephone sales representative in the customer relationship management system, and contact options the customer can select online. Alerts are pushed out via text, phone call, or email — again, by customer choice.

When it's time to consider a new machine, or the customer has growth plans, the telephone salesperson alerts a field sales representative who has a considerably larger territory, and rarely visits a customer unless they're in the market for a new machine. When the field salesperson arrives, the customer has already educated themselves online, and the discussions are less on the features of a new machine than on productivity (how much can be moved in an hour), safety (what can be done to prevent accidents) and cost-per-hour (fuel usage, maintenance costs and resale value). The machines themselves are really a commodity, and the differentiation between suppliers is minor.

- What does this dealer offer? A product or a service? Which is more important to building customer loyalty and repeat sales?
- Is the telephone sales representative part of the sales channel or communication channel? Or both?
- Where would you locate this telephone sales representative, in the sales department or marketing department?

The telephone salesperson in the example above spends most of her time in the first three consulting elements of our sales model, DISCOVER, DESIGN, and DEMONSTRATE, rather than in the fourth and fifth sales steps, CLOSE and CHECK. Technology enables the telephone sales rep to cover a broad territory, and yet technology provides her with the tools to deepen and broaden the relationship. The customer interacts with the dealer on mobile and desktop platforms.

The National Center for Biotechnological Information shows the average human attention span has dropped from 12 seconds in 2000 to 8 seconds in 2013. However, the telephone salesperson in this example has at least four quality 10-minute phone conversations a year — and more when data warrants it. The dealer relies on technology for the large service component of its offering, but the telephone sales rep supplies the high touch.

The goal for many business-to-business suppliers is to create a consistent customer experience — mobile, online, inside the service or product factory, and on the phone. Critically, the messaging, pricing, and information delivered must be consistent. The telephone sales rep in the modern era must ask customers what the most appropriate touch points are, and customize the selling organization's delivery of touch points in conjunction with their marketing departments.

The telephone rep is both a communication and sales channel. As the primary customer-facing individual from the selling organization, the telephone rep establishes the appropriate communication mechanisms, and builds the relationship — probing for the customer's business opportunities and strategies which would otherwise be opaque to the selling organization. The telephone sales rep is a consultant, understanding the customer's business to the extent necessary to recommend the appropriate products and services, while also diagnosing and assuring any customer service issues are resolved.

Because the telephone sales rep occupies this critical boundary position between the customer and the selling organization, they have communication responsibilities in both directions — to the customer and back to the organization. Some of the organizational communication requirements are routine, including checking the "Do Not Mail" box in the customer relationship management system (CRM), assuring all the contact information including email and mobile numbers are correct, and helping the customer set up their links to the selling organization's information systems. Others are more complex, including communicating nuanced service requirements, smoothing over invoicing disputes, or going to bat for a customer who needs quick credit approval.

The telephone sales rep closes business of course, navigating the buying committee, matching needs to benefits, cross- and up-selling, and translating the obscure technical specifications of the selling organization to the customer's language. Perhaps most importantly, the telephone salesperson addresses risk — both indirectly and directly. As customer's information gathering becomes more digital, and attention spans decrease. Customers need assurance they have interpreted information correctly and are making good decisions.

After all, customers are not only managing the digital information coming from the selling organization, but from competitors and a myriad of other suppliers. The telephone salesperson, because he or she is familiar with the organization, and has asked enough questions to understand the customer's opportunities and strategies, is a trusted resource and sounding board. This relationship reduces risk indirectly. The salesperson addresses risk directly by probing during the sales cycle, and adding steps into the sales process designed to address elements of risk.

The telephone salesperson performs both marketing and sales functions. Because marketing traditionally owns the brand, and today the brand is the total customer experience, the salesperson not only creates part of the experience directly through dialogue, he or she asks questions which help shape and customize future marketing communications. Together with a customer's online behavior, the information obtained by the salesperson is used to tailor the selling organization's message to each customer's unique needs.

The marketing department of today's business-to-business selling organization can work with the telephone sales group to prepare custom personal messages that can be sent between telephone contacts, leveraging the relationship, and keeping the customer contact warm. In many organizations, the telephone salespeople also staff the chat function connected to the selling organization's website, assisting existing customers with questions, and supporting prospects in their journey to learn more about the selling organization.

I opened this chapter with an example of a forklift dealer and asked the question, is the dealer selling a product or service or both? The dealer is selling a customer experience. This customer experience contains a product, a host of services to support the product, digital communications in several formats, and the human connection provided by the telephone sales rep. Twenty years ago, the dealer would have been a forklift dealer. Today the dealer is the customer's "material handling partner." Most of the value added is contained in the services which support the product, and the services flow seamlessly digitally from the customer to the dealer and back again. The telephone salesperson provides the human element, less in charge of managing the day-to-day, which technology does mostly on its own, but in catching problems before they become show stoppers. Most critically, the telephone salesperson is tasked with keeping tabs on the customer's opportunities and strategies, to fine tune the selling organization's service and product offerings to match.

Since the release of the smart phone in June of 2007, I have seen a steady increase in the skill set necessary to be a good telephone salesperson in the business-to-business space. The consulting role enabled by technology, the blend of services and product, and the tailoring of marketing messaging have changed the job since the days of just smiling and dialing. The distance between the telemarketer and the business-to-business salesperson just keeps widening.

Chapter 29
Your Journey

I was sitting in the conference room with a prospective client and his team, and he motioned the door shut. "Okay," he said. "So, you've told us how you could help us. But tell me, what can go wrong? What are the biggest mistakes you've seen people do with business-to-business telephone sales?" Now this is a loaded question from a potential client you are just getting to know. You may mention a common mistake only to find out later it is something they've tried.

You don't know who the sponsor was — some other consultant who has been kicked to the curb (and therefore it is okay to disparage their once-great idea), or maybe the boss sponsored it, or perhaps someone in the room. I gave them this response: "The biggest challenges I've seen are: 1) Being influenced too strongly by what you think you know, 2) Failure to create a bullet-proof business model, 3) Not balancing marketing and sales, 4) Not putting a great manager in place, and finally, 5) Not establishing a sales culture where your team can be successful."

The manager turned to me and said, "We've done a few of those things."

I said, "If I tried to make your product or deliver your services, I'd never be able to make it work. Telephone selling is not intuitive, just like making your product or delivering your service is not intuitive."

In business-to-business sales, we often take our superior knowledge of our business, and our small information about the customer to create a "selling intuition." We design marketing pieces, promotional campaigns, advertising and personal selling strategies, all based on our superior knowledge of our business and our estimates of what it's like to be a customer. Our telephone salespeople make calls with superior inside knowledge, and our public relations departments churn out internal releases about our business. We know everything about our business.

The customer, however, lives in a different world. Their own unique world. In the customer's world, your business is a fleeting intersection in the universe of vendors, a temporary solution to one of endless parade of never-ending problems — a distraction on a busy day. In the world of the customer, they don't think about your business very often. If you disappear, well, most of the time they'll find someone else.

Replicating the customer's world inside a sales department requires that you set aside your superior inside knowledge and focus on information and a frank and realistic appraisal of experience. What works, what doesn't, what has been tested and proven, and what has not.

Unfortunately, in the context of this current discussion, the entrepreneur that established your business or the professional manager that runs it probably has a passion for the organization. After all, entrepreneurs survive the slings and arrows of outrageous fortune by a true belief the organization is superior, the product or service is the best, and the opportunities are legion.

The professional manager, often the workaholic, defines much of who he or she is by the job — by the company. These folks are long on inside experience and short on knowing what it's like to be a customer. How can they truly know what it's like to be a customer? Their day-to-day experiences can't help but give them a clouded view — a view tainted by the inside knowledge they own.

The same holds true for telephone sales. Many sales training processes revolve around bathing the telephone salesperson in insider knowledge. They spend time on the shop floor, or "service factory" or wherever it is that you make what you do. If your organization is selling consulting, they talk to consultants. If your organization is distributing products, they talk to the producers. This type of training is valuable and cannot be discounted. Salespeople must represent the product or service and must be an expert.

What is missing often, however, is the immersion in what it's like to be a customer. If you are selling tables, has the salesperson spent time setting up a convention floor full of tables for a large banquet? If you are a retailer, has the salesperson gone out and bought something from your competitors?

Often in this book, I have mentioned the power of positioning, of trying multiple approaches and call outlines within different customer segments to see what works best to begin the relationship and to introduce new products or services into existing relationships. I have been surprised on numerous occasions on what positioning ends up working best. Often with clients we'll go to the white board and brainstorm a variety of positions to test, and I'll take a vote around the room on the favorite. Rarely does the favorite win, because those of us in the room have too much information which clouds our choices.

A definite risk in business-to-business telephone selling is having too much reliance on the brilliance of the salespeople hired, and too little on the thought and preparation of designing the sales system within which they will work. Selection is critical, the goal being to find the best individuals with the best attributes for the job. But even the best selected salesperson will fall short if they are just handed a list of prospects or customers and told to do their best. Recognize that your most expensive asset and cost center is the payroll of the person who puts the headset on and is making calls. All the training, and all the dollars invested in designing the best sales system, pale against the payroll cost which ticks on and on, like an expensive metronome — every payroll period.

Second, look at your business model. Make sure the math makes sense. With the telephone salesperson reaching customers around 20% of the time per dial, can they complete enough activities in a day to generate the revenue needed to support the position? Calculate the cost-of-sales and the cost-of-marketing, and make sure the resulting business model works with your cost-of-goods sold (product) or cost-of-delivery (services).

Third, look at your marketing. If the telephone salespeople will be prospecting, what can marketing do to generate leads to minimize cold calling? Personal selling is often the most expensive way to prospect. Is there something marketing can do to get people to raise their hands and say "I'm at least mildly interested?" If not, can marketing help segment the prospect list into those most likely to be receptive because of demographic or psychographic criteria? Within the prospect list, can management design a strategy to test positioning so the sales group can hone in on the best approach to each segment? Rejigger the business model, if necessary, as you adjust the marketing investment. In many of our clients' business models, the cost-of-sales and cost-of-marketing are within the same ballpark.

Fourth, look at sales management. Some former salespeople may not be the best managers. They may focus more on helping their salespeople close deals and less on the design, operation, and management of an effective sales system. They may be frustrated because their salespeople are not up to their personal skill level, and may then rely on taking over deals rather than coaching each representative how to do it themselves. It takes a true dedication to performance management to realize the best leverage a manager has is to develop a telephone sales team who can pursue and close business on their own, to coach rather than to take it over. It is also hard to do the hundreds of tasks each day which incrementally make the department more effective.

The average telephone sales manager has an effective span of control over eight salespeople. To keep a high-performing team of eight, the sales manager must be hiring to keep the team filled, orienting new representatives, arranging training — both in product and services and in sales skills — and managing and leading the group. The sales manager must also be able to relate to the rest of the organization and to represent the sales group to other departments. This is especially true in organizations selling services, because the customer influences the consumption of the service.

Finally, establish a good sales culture. If a sales manager rolls out a Personal Business Plan with activity goals attached, and the manager does not measure and report back actual activities, it is likely the number of activities performed over time will diminish. If a telephone representative is sitting in a cubicle, and the person sitting next to them is doing 50 dials a day, not the 60 in their plan, it is likely their performance will slide down to the performance of the person sitting next to them. When a new person joins the department, they will quickly pick up on the norms of the group and adopt them, because they don't want to stand out, and they sense that this is what it takes to get along and go along within the sales department.

A high-performing sales department will make an incoming representative perform to the best of their ability. An under-performing sales department will tend to dampen an incoming representative and the organization will get less than they deserve. A high-performance sales culture is instituted with a compensation plan that is fair and easily understood, with Personal Business Plans achievable with superior effort, storytelling to build group cohesiveness, and one-on-one coaching. If your organization selects salespeople with the right aptitude for the job, provides them with onboarding and training, and immerses them within a high-performing culture, a good business model will be executable.

I've seen telephone sales departments where the sales manager rings a bell for each major accomplishment. Some managers put large pictures of high performers in high-traffic areas where everyone can see them. Others offer trips or even afternoons off to spend additional time with their families. Many things can work, but the job of being on the phone and getting no answer and "not interested" many more times than "yes" can be draining. Don't forget the emotional nutrition. It is the high-energy snack food of great sales culture.

Today is a wonderful time to consider a business-to-business telephone selling effort. Security concerns reduce customer visiting access, business travel continues to get more expensive, and the smartphone makes reaching a specific decision maker easier. This device in the palm of your customer's hand enables your organization to push information right where it is needed, and a salesperson who can call and explain it all. As the power of marketing automation grows, the human voice over the phone will become more and more integrated with marketing messages, creating the opportunity for stronger, deeper, and more meaningful relationships.

We started this book by contrasting and comparing relationship-based telephone selling and telemarketing. With the technology available to us today to pinpoint needs, customize target emails, and follow people around the web with adverts, why is building human relationships with business customers important?

Why go through all this work? Because the human being who is your buyer still craves being in a business relationship with someone from your organization who cares. Someone who is willing to meet them halfway, who is concerned about their business, not just the next transaction. Any substantial purchase your buyer makes is still gut-wrenching at some level. It still involves risk. Your buyer is going out on a limb, politically. It is vital for you to have someone out on the branch to make it seem less stressful.

Just because you are good at making a product or delivering a service, doesn't automatically give you the knowledge on the best way to go to market. Everyone needs to test to see what works — not work what you think.

But then again ... you don't need to use intuition for your journey. You've read at least one book.

FIVE-STEP ADVANCED SOLUTION
SELLING MODEL

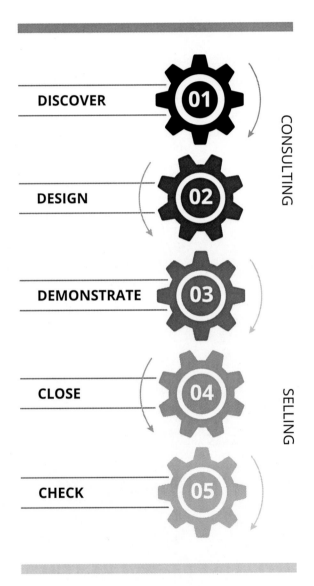

DISCOVER — 01

DESIGN — 02

DEMONSTRATE — 03

CLOSE — 04

CHECK — 05

CONSULTING

SELLING

About Business Performance Group

Founded in 2000, Business Performance Group provides consulting and training to organizations using open-dialogue telephone selling business-to-business. Our clients are diverse, from construction equipment manufacturers to medical rehabilitation service providers, but each client is dedicated to creating an ongoing annuity stream from their customer base.

Business Performance Group's consulting strategy focuses on helping organizations establish a unique business model and deployment plan suited to their specific customer and market challenges. We work with marketing departments to design lead generation programs and target email campaigns to support a telephone sales effort. We work with human resources to design a selection process fine-tuned to hire the best candidate. And we work with sales managers to design metrics and dashboards to lead and manage their teams, and integrate open-dialogue telephone sales with other platforms, such as field sales.

Our first level of training curricula is designed for the manager. Our programs progressively advance from business model creation, to sales-employee selection, onboarding, training, coaching, managing and leading. The goal is for the manager to not only learn how to run a successful department, but to leave the training session with the documents and plans necessary for execution.

Our second level of training is designed for the telephone sales representative who is building relationships over the phone. This training is based on a five-step model: DISCOVER, DESIGN, DEMONSTRATE, CLOSE and CHECK. Participants learn not only how to sell, but how to build relationships incrementally, one call at a time. As a prerequisite to onsite training, we offer nineteen interactive online course modules around each aspect of the job. This allows new representatives to learn their craft in easily digestible sessions, and allows the manager to coach effectively by referring their salespeople back to specific modules as a refresher.

Business
■Performance Group

www.BPGrp.com

Index

A

Acknowledge 147
Across the Table 6, 163
ACT 141
Action 115, 116, 118
Aptitudes 106, 120
attributes 25, 26, 43, 45, 46, 48, 51, 63, 120, 193

B

Bill Buss 5, 19, 29, 39, 67, 79, 105, 110, 117, 143, 164
Bob Morrison 14, 20, 79, 133
body language 10, 20, 91, 95, 137, 158, 182
brush off 147
business curiosity 10, 34, 35, 36, 38, 48, 85
Business Development Plan 120
business issue 13, 21, 23, 24, 25, 28, 41, 43, 45, 46, 48, 49, 54, 61, 63, 69, 73, 75, 82, 83, 84, 85, 87, 88, 89, 117, 125, 154, 157
business issues 10, 17, 21, 22, 32, 35, 61, 74, 84, 87, 116, 151
business partnership 37, 38
Business Performance Group 1, 2, 7, 9, 10, 15, 21, 27, 28, 69, 83, 113, 143, 144, 164, 177, 184, 197
business proposal 52, 53, 86, 157, 158, 159, 161, 162

business relationship 15, 31, 32, 33, 35, 41, 73, 81, 157, 195
business relationships 7, 9, 15, 17, 33, 36, 45
business-to-business 7, 9, 11, 15, 16, 18, 21, 24, 28, 31, 32, 33, 35, 43, 52, 54, 79, 84, 85, 97, 100, 121, 123, 140, 157, 167, 169, 177, 182, 187, 188, 189, 191, 193, 194, 197
buying committee 45, 46, 50, 52, 85, 88, 95, 117, 139, 140, 170, 174, 178, 187
buying cycle 17, 23, 24, 26, 41, 43

C

Caliper 14, 68, 93, 108
call outline 85, 147, 148
call outlines 101, 102, 103, 192
Call Outlines 53
CHECK 6, 17, 109, 112, 177, 178, 179
CLOSE 5, 6, 17, 109, 112, 137, 147, 157
closed-ended question 51, 78, 157, 158, 159
Commitment 115, 119
compelling reason to call 60, 62, 63, 64, 77, 78, 87, 147, 149, 150, 177, 179
compensation 49, 50, 72, 73, 109, 128, 129, 170, 194
Competencies 106
consultant 16, 19, 39, 51, 52, 65, 81, 96, 143, 164, 168, 171, 187, 191

Contracting 115
CRM 17, 29, 187
customer narrative 17, 33, 35, 40, 60, 62, 63, 175, 178
customer service 14, 17, 20, 29, 37, 47, 59, 62, 84, 89, 104, 106, 110, 123, 125, 177, 178, 179, 181, 182, 187

D

DEMONSTRATE 5, 17, 83, 95, 109, 112
DESIGN 5, 16, 17, 43, 59, 71, 109, 112
DISCOVER 5, 16, 17, 21, 31, 48, 61, 63, 109, 112

E

emotional labor 100, 102, 120, 122, 126, 129
emotional nutrition 33, 69, 100, 102, 121, 126, 128, 194
empathy 34, 68, 105, 120

F

field salesperson 9, 13, 16, 17, 18, 32, 36, 53, 59, 68, 95, 100, 104, 186

G

gatekeeper 60, 61, 80, 149, 150, 151

H

heterogeneity 167, 168, 173
HRDQ 2, 181

Istanbul, which in biblical times was called Constantinople. In February 1971, Eddie and Pearl's marriage ended in divorce. Washington's tour of duty, in the summer of 1971, was a three-year stint at Fort Meade, Maryland, where he met his fiancée, Mary Moses. At the National Cryptologic School, he was the Chief Instructor for the Basic Signals Intelligence Course where he taught the physics of electromagnetic wave propagation, interception, and analysis. He lived in Laurel, Maryland, which is 18 miles from both Baltimore and Washington, D.C.

En route to Germany in June 1977, Washington married his fiancée, Mary Moses. Then Eddie reported to duty at Ida Oberstein, near Baumholder, Germany, where he served as an Emanations Analysis Technician and Unit Training Coordinator. The author and his wife travelled extensively through Europe including the countries of Germany, England, France, Belgium, Netherlands, Luxembourg, and Spain, which included watching a bull fight. However, the highlight of this period for Mary and Eddie was their vacation to Egypt, Jordan, and Israel. He also earned a Master of Science Degree in Business Administration from Boston University.

From 1984 to 2013, Eddie Washington worked for defense contractor, which primarily supports Department of Defense customers nationwide. During his career there, Eddie grew from staff member to project manager to program manager and finally to subcontracts manager. He took advantage of many interesting opportunities, including travel to Puerto Rico, Guam, Hawaii and Spain. He and his wife live in Southern Maryland and have three grown sons, Duane, Edward and Eric. Eddie plans to write more books and short stories.

21496837R00143

Made in the USA
Charleston, SC
22 August 2013